The Boy in the Song

The Boy in the Song

THE TRUE STORIES
BEHIND 50 ROCK CLASSICS

MICHAEL HEATLEY & FRANK HOPKINSON

CHICAGO
REVIEW
PRESS

An A Cappella Book

This edition published in 2012 by Chicago Review Press, Incorporated
First published in the United Kingdom in 2012 by Portico Books
An imprint of Anova Books Company Ltd
10 Southcombe Street, London W14 0RA

Chicago Review Press, Incorporated
814 North Franklin Street
Chicago, Illinois 60610
ISBN 978-1-61374-331-7
5 4 3 2 1

Cover image: Corbis
Back cover image: Jeff Buckley (Getty Images)
Page 2: Sid Vicious (Rex Features)

Reproduction by Rival Colour Ltd.
Printed and bound by Everbest Printing, China

Contents

Amazing
George Michael

As part of British pop duo Wham! in the 1980s, George Michael adorned the bedroom walls of countless teenage girls across Britain. But continuing questions about his sexuality were answered when police caught him performing a lewd act in a Los Angeles park toilet in 1998. The scandal confirmed Michael's sexuality in the most public of ways.

Two years before the incident in the summer of 1996 Michael had begun dating US businessman Kenny Goss. The pair were together at the time of the police sting, but such was the nature of their relationship that the scandal caused more of a stir among the world's media than it did between George and Kenny. Goss remembered the moment in an interview with US

Kenny Goss with George Michael at Elle Macpherson's birthday bash in 1999.

talk-show host Oprah Winfrey: "He called me and said, 'You are not going to believe what I've done.' Got a DUI [Driving Under the Influence]? He goes, "If only …'"

George often praised Kenny for his understanding of his flamboyant nature and that tolerance helped strengthen their relationship over the years. "We've had our problems but he's never had a problem with my lifestyle," was George's take on it. Kenny's lenience and acceptance is displayed in "Amazing," George's tribute to his boyfriend, where he sings:

> You tried to save me from myself
> Said 'Darling, kiss as many as you want!'

His appreciation of Goss perhaps reflects the fact that they met when

George was at his lowest after losing his mother to cancer. George's feelings are reflected in the song's opening lyrics: "I was mixed up when you came to me, too broke to fix."

The glowing acknowledgment of his partner was released in 2004 after the dust surrounding the 1998 scandal had long since settled. "Amazing" soared to the Top 5 in the UK as fans showed their approval of the dance-influenced number. The album it came from, *Patience*, performed even better, topping the UK charts and hitting #12 in the US Billboard 200.

Sadly, George announced from the stage at the start of his Symphonica tour at the State Opera House in Prague in August 2011 that he was no longer with his long-term partner. "In truth, Kenny and I have not been together for two and a half years," he told fans, his voice breaking with emotion. He said he was sorry for any pain he had caused his former partner, adding he thought it was better to be honest about the real situation: "This man has brought me a lot of joy and a lot of pain. The truth is my love life has been a lot more turbulent than I've let on … I'm so sad about my relationship with Kenny," he added.

He then introduced a new track, "Where I Hope You Are," which had been inspired by the split.

GEORGE MICHAEL, of Greek-Cypriot heritage, was born Giorgios Panayiotou in London in 1963. He emerged from teen duo Wham! in the mid 1980s and went on to conquer the American market in 1987 with his first solo album *Faith*. A battle with record label Sony raged until 1995, clearing the way for the introspective album *Older*.

In 2006 Michael started his first tour in 15 years, performing in 41 countries to two million fans. The last years of the decade were more notable for run-ins with the law over soft and prescription drug use, but he maintained his public profile through use of the social medium of Twitter.

Andy's Chest
Lou Reed

Pop artist and commercial illustrator Andy Warhol founded his legendary New York studio, the Factory, in 1962. It soon became the "in"place for artists, musicians, and bohemians to hang out. By 1965, Warhol had turned his attention to moviemaking and music. The Velvet Underground, led by Lou Reed, entered his orbit via an associate. He became their manager and, in return for funding the band, Warhol insisted that one of his protégés, German model Nico, join as additional vocalist. The band toured America as part of Warhol's *Exploding Plastic Inevitable*, a multimedia extravaganza also featuring dancing, film, and performance art.

The Velvets with Andy Warhol: (L-R) Nico, Warhol, Yule, Reed, Morrison, and Cale (seated).

Reed acknowledged Warhol's pivotal role in the Velvet Underground's early career. "We were doing our shows and we weren't even making enough to put the show on next day and Andy would go and do commercial art things constantly just to get the money together to put on the show. That's how we stayed together. It was all down to Andy."

Nominally, Warhol produced their first album *The Velvet Underground and Nico*, and designed the famous "banana" cover. Toward the end of 1967, when Warhol had seemingly lost interest in the band, Reed ousted him as manager.

On June 3, 1968, Warhol was shot at the Factory by the radical feminist Valerie Solanas, a small player in the Factory scene who suffered from the delusion that Warhol was controlling her and that to free herself she must kill him. The artist suffered life-threatening injuries to his chest and, although he recovered, the assassination attempt left physical and mental scars. "Before I was shot, I always thought that I was more half-there than all-there—I always suspected that I was watching TV instead of living life. People sometimes say that the way things happen in movies is unreal, but actually it's the way things happen in life that's unreal. The movies make emotions look so strong and real, whereas when things really do happen to you it's like watching television—you don't feel anything. Right when I was being shot and ever since, I knew that I was watching television. The channels switch, but it's all television."

Despite Warhol's firing, Reed wrote "Andy's Chest" shortly afterward as a goodwill message to Warhol. "It's what I thought about Andy being shot," said Reed. "It's about that, even though the lyrics don't sound like it." He also claimed that "It's a love song." The original 1968 Velvet Underground version was not released until 1985 on *VU,* a collection of outtakes. Reed refashioned "Andy's Chest" for his 1972 album *Transformer,* produced by David Bowie and guitarist Mick Ronson.

Warhol died after a gall bladder operation in 1987. As well as coining the aphorism "in the future everyone will be famous for 15 minutes," Warhol is part of an elite group of artists whose work has sold for $100 million. His screen prints of a Campbell's soup can and Marilyn Monroe are among the best known artworks of the twentieth century.

LOU REED was the principal songwriter of the Velvet Underground, one of the most influential rock bands of all time. Reed's second album, *Transformer,* made him a household name with the hit single "Walk on the Wild Side," which, like "Andy's Chest" and much of the material on the album, was inspired by Warhol's Factory.

Reed collaborated with John Cale on the biographical *Songs for Drella,* Warhol's nickname, after his death in 1987. The Velvet Underground reformed briefly in 1993. "Perfect Day" from *Transformer* became an unlikely standard when used as a UK charity single in 1997.

Back on the Chain Gang
The Pretenders

It's remarkable that such a bright, uptempo pop song should emerge from the circumstances behind the creation of the Pretenders' hit "Back on the Chain Gang." But on closer investigation, the lyrics hint at the birth, death, addiction, and betrayal that surround it.

The Pretenders formed in 1978 to perform the songs of singer and sometime journalist Chrissie Hynde. Their first hit, however, was a version of "Stop Your Sobbing" by Hynde's songwriting idol, Kinks' frontman Ray Davies. Davies had led the iconic British pop band since 1964, and Hynde met him at last in 1980 during a US tour. They began an offstage relationship, in the course of which Ray left his wife to be with Chrissie. By May 1982 they were expecting a child together.

It was to prove a stormy relationship. Plans to marry were called off when they began arguing so intensely before the proposed ceremony that, according to Davies, the registrar refused to conduct it. Hynde began to write the song that would become "Back on the Chain Gang" when she looked at the photo of him she kept in her purse:

> I found a picture of you
> … Now we're back in the fight.

After a run of single chart successes, two big-selling albums, and a series of world tours, the rock'n'roll lifestyle was beginning to take its toll on the band. On June 14, 1982 Hynde fired bassist Pete Farndon (with whom she had earlier had an affair) for belligerence and unreliability caused by excessive drug use. Two days later, both the band and their fans were stunned by news of the death of the Pretenders' guitarist James Honeyman-Scott from a cocaine overdose.

"He really was the Pretenders' sound," recalled Chrissie. "I don't sound like that." Scott's death shook Hynde profoundly. The British press descended on her in a frenzy at the whiff of another drug-fueled pop scandal. As in the song: "The phone, the TV, and the *News of the World* descended like flies" and she took refuge in her work.

The lyrics she was working on changed direction, becoming less about Davies and more about "Jimmy Scott," his importance in the band, and

Ray Davies of the Kinks performing live in 1980. Ray enjoyed a tempestuous relationship with brother Dave onstage and Chrissie Hynde offstage.

the pressures of pop success that drive performers to excess. Barely a month later, on July 20, the pregnant Hynde took a scratch version of the Pretenders' line-up into the studio to record the song. The hastily recruited musicians included guitarists Robbie McIntosh (Scott's own recommendation to augment the band's sound) and Billy Bremner, who came up with the

A rare fan pic of Ray and Chrissie together in the early 1980s with Brian Hibbard (right).

distinctive solo on the finished recording.

Bremner began his career in Lulu's backing band the Luvvers in 1966, and more recently he had been a member of Rockpile, whose leader Dave Edmunds inspired Scott's multilayered guitar sound. To complete the link of this particular chain, bass player Nick Lowe had produced the Pretenders' version of Ray Davies' "Stop Your Sobbing."

When "Back on the Chain Gang" was released in October 1982, fans celebrated it as a tribute to the band's late guitarist. When sacked bassist Farndon also succumbed to drugs in April 1983, drowning in his bath after a heroin overdose, the themes of the song took on an even deeper resonance.

Chrissie Hynde's life was no less turbulent after "Back on the Chain Gang" than it had been before it. The song had barely left the charts when, in January 1983, she gave birth to Natalie, her daughter with Davies. Both parents continued to tour with their respective bands, occasionally (when tempers permitted) guesting with each other's. Hynde insisted on taking Natalie with her on the road.

In January 1984 the Pretenders' world tour coincided briefly, at two festivals in New South Wales, Australia, with that of Simple Minds. In an echo of her history with Ray Davies, she began an affair with the Simple Minds' singer Jim Kerr. By May of that year she had married Kerr.

The birth of Yasmin, Hynde and Kerr's daughter, in 1987 coincided with a period of inactivity for the Pretenders. But when her marriage to Kerr ended in 1990, Hynde picked up the reins once again. The Pretenders tour and record to this day, with the frontwoman as firmly in control of the band's line-up and direction as she always was.

Following the end of his relationship with Hynde, Ray Davies took refuge in his work, writing and directing a TV film *Return to Waterloo* and its soundtrack, his first solo album. He continued to lead the Kinks until they disbanded in 1996 and has toured regularly since as a solo performer and raconteur.

Despite having left his wife to be with Chrissie, Ray remains very bitter about Chrissie's departure from him to be with Jim Kerr. They have not spoken since, although he did invite the Pretenders to perform the Kinks' hit "Waterloo Sunset" when the latter were inducted into the UK Music Hall of Fame in 2005.

But in 2009 the parents were reunited, after a fashion, thanks to the go-between efforts of their daughter Natalie. Ray and Chrissie sang together on a Christmas charity single released that year, "Postcards from London." It was Natalie who brought the song to her mother's attention. But her father was at pains, when promoting the single, to distance himself from his former partner. He made it clear that they did not meet face to face, and that she overdubbed her part separately in the studio. "It wasn't recorded around a log fire or anything," he emphasized in an interview for the *Independent* newspaper. "She wasn't my first choice. I wanted [veteran British 1940s troop entertainer] Dame Vera Lynn."

For her part, Hynde claimed "I'd rather shoot myself than sing 'Back on the Chain Gang'" when playing an internet broadcast session for AOL. Unlike Davies, she did, however, relent.

THE PRETENDERS combined the talents of three British musicians—bassist Pete Farndon, guitarist James Honeyman-Scott, and drummer Martin Chambers with American frontwoman and songwriter Chrissie Hynde. The 1979 UK chart-topping success of single "Brass in Pocket" would prove their peak just a year after forming, as the loss of Farndon and Honeyman-Scott in drug-related deaths destroyed the original quartet.

Hynde has kept the group going to the present day, occasionally with the assistance of Chambers, and remains a potent songwriter and performer. When her band was inducted into the Rock and Roll Hall of Fame in 2005, she said "I know that the Pretenders have looked like a tribute band for the last 20 years. ... And we're paying tribute to James Honeyman-Scott and Pete Farndon, without whom we wouldn't be here."

Back to Black

Amy Winehouse

"**B**ack to Black" is a song that not only defined a relationship but came to define a troubled yet brilliant artist. It was the title track from one of the most critically acclaimed albums of a generation and, enormously popular upon its release in 2006, received a new lease of life in tragic circumstances five years later. Yet for all its popularity, "Back to Black" displayed the turmoil and torment of an unhealthy relationship, and a disturbed life that would ultimately claim the life of its creator, Amy Winehouse.

Though she became known just as much for her battle with her drink and drug demons as her music, it was her vocal talent that initially brought Winehouse to the attention of the masses. Seen as a trailblazer for the modern female artist, she achieved transatlantic recognition, something that had become hard to come by after the 1990s proved a barren decade in terms of British female success in the U.S.

Debut album *Frank* was not a global chart-topper yet displayed a fresh-faced Amy singing largely about an ex-love. It was a hit in her home country, initially charting in the Top 20 and being nominated for the Mercury Music Prize. But the album *Back to Black*, released in October 2006, saw a reinvented Winehouse come at the public from a totally different angle, complete with (soon-to-be) trademark beehive hairdo. And while the new look and more soulful sound was exciting, it indicated a personal change that would ultimately define the rest of her life.

While the hit single "Rehab" is regularly touted as Amy's defining song after her own well-documented trips to rehabilitation facilities, "Back to Black" provided a more intimate glimpse into her feelings. The jazz-infused ballad was the third single from the multi award-winning album and arrived in April 2007, after the success of "Rehab" and "You Know I'm No Good," while her behavior was beginning to land her on the front pages of the tabloids.

Amy Winehouse had met Blake Fielder-Civil, who worked in TV production, in 2005 and reportedly fell into drugs almost immediately. Fielder-Civil later admitted his regrets over his role. "I made the biggest mistake of my life by taking heroin in front of her. I introduced her to heroin, crack cocaine, and self-harming. I feel more than guilty."

The pair's on-off relationship spawned the majority of *Back to Black*, including the title track where Amy grieves over her beau returning to his ex-girlfriend. "We only said goodbye with words—I died a hundred times," she sings. The lyric showed the impact Blake had on her life even in the early days of their affair.

She told CNN of the inspiration for the track: "It's about being in a relationship that, when it's finished, you go back to what you know. Except I wasn't working so I couldn't throw myself into my job, so when the guy I was seeing went back to his ex-girlfriend I didn't have anything

Amy Winehouse and her trademark beehive, shooting a video in Los Angeles with husband Blake Fielder-Civil in May 2007.

to go back to. So I went back to a very black few months doing silly things, as you do when you're 22 and in love."

Though Amy didn't go into detail about those "silly things," the song's lyrics display the true extent of her fractured yet intense relationship with Fielder-Civil, and referenced the drugs that would continue to dominate her life. Amy cries "I love you (so) much, it's not enough—you love blow and I love puff." While many would say she was still firmly in control of her life at that point, the signs of her fall into the damaging world of narcotics were evident.

Their reconciliation after the album's release made it somewhat awkward when singing the lyrics live, a situation Amy herself conceded was "weird." But being reunited didn't dent the poignant nature of the tracks and Amy carried on regardless. She told an audience in 2007: "We went on our little separate ways, but then realized that we loved each other. Life's too short." Amy later reflected on their breakup before writing *Back to Black*: "[Blake] and I did the most horrible things that two

AMY WINEHOUSE ensured herself a place in the "27 club" alongside Hendrix, Cobain, Morrison, and others when she departed this life in July 2011. Claims that she was "Britain's Aretha Franklin" were risible given only two albums' worth of released material (a third was in the process of being rerecorded in periods when she was fit to do so), but there's no doubt she laid greater claim to Janis Joplin parallels in that her demise was widely predicted and her songs seemed fuelled by her personal misery and despair. While debut album *Frank* earned a Mercury Music Prize nomination, *Back to Black* brought home six Grammy Award nominations and five wins, equalling the then record for the most wins by a female artist in a single night. Her album received the most coveted award—Record of the Year. It was a stratospheric rise, for which she paid the ultimate price.

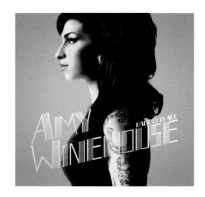

people in love could do to each other. I think it was a case of we met too young, and we weren't prepared for the way that we felt about each other. It was too much—it burnt out."

But the flame didn't burn out with Blake. The pair got back together as the success of *Back to Black* soared, and eventually married in May 2007. But their two-year union was dogged by tabloid tales of fights and drug-taking, and when Blake was imprisoned in 2008, events in Amy's life nosedived.

However, as soon as Fielder-Civil emerged from Her Majesty's Pleasure at the beginning of 2009, the marriage fell apart as he filed for divorce, citing adultery after Amy was pictured with another man while on vacation.

The "relatively" good times: strolling together in New York, August 2007.

But Blake would play a major role in the rest of Amy's life, albeit not always in a direct capacity. Though he would meet a new partner—in rehab, of all places—and Amy would later link up with British actor Reg Traviss, the pair seemingly retained a connection as rumors of late-night messaging abounded.

Amy Winehouse was found dead in her Camden apartment in July 2011. The initial cause of death was unclear, but by October 26, 2011 the coroner could report that it was alcohol poisoning and not drugs that had taken her life. Though divorced for nearly two years, Blake spoke from prison of his devastation to UK tabloid *The Sun*: "I'm beyond inconsolable … my tears won't dry. I will never ever again feel the love I felt for her. Everybody who knew me and knew Amy knew the depth of our love. I can't believe she's dead."

While her fans and critics alike lamented the loss of a life with so much talent and potential, Amy's lyrics continued to resonate: "And I tread a troubled track, my odds are stacked—I'll go back to black."

Bobby Jean
Bruce Springsteen

It would be easy to assume that "Bobby Jean" is a song about the end of a relationship with a girlfriend: that Bruce Springsteen is breaking up with a lover. Yet the name—half male, half female—is deliberately ambiguous and Springsteen has described the song as being "about youthful friendship."

The friend in question is in fact Steve Van Zandt, guitarist with Springsteen's E Street Band and long-time collaborator and confidant of the singer. The two men grew up together in New Jersey; Van Zandt played in Springsteen's early group Steel Mill and soon found they "liked the same music … liked the same bands … liked the same clothes."

When Springsteen secured a recording contract in 1972, he cherry-picked members of the New Jersey scene to become the E Street Band. Van Zandt, otherwise engaged, did not join until 1975 while the band were touring *Born to Run,* although he contributed in the sessions for the album, giving "the Boss" his opinion in his typically forthright fashion. "All I did on *Born to Run* were the horns on '10th Avenue Freeze-Out.' I was just in the studio, hanging around. He said, 'What do you think?' and I said, 'I think it sucks.' And he said, 'Well, go fucking fix it, then. So I went and fixed it.'"

"Bobby Jean" represents Springsteen's farewell to Van Zandt who left the E Street Band after recording *Born in the USA* in 1984.

> And I'm just calling one last time not to change your mind
> But just to say I miss you, baby, good luck, goodbye, Bobby Jean

Nicknamed "Miami" Steve by Springsteen, Van Zandt was and remains a songwriter and producer in his own right, his work with New Jersey outfit Southside Johnny and the Asbury Jukes of particular note. After leaving the E Street Band, his highest-profile project was the 1985 Artists United Against Apartheid single "Sun City," to which a multitude of big names, Springsteen included, contributed. The aim of the song was to raise awareness about the apartheid regime in South Africa. Van Zandt also fronted his own occasional band Little Steven and the Disciples of Soul, recording four albums under that banner.

Although he had no previous acting experience, Van Zandt took on a major role as Silvio Dante in the acclaimed television drama *The Sopranos* in 1999. He was highly praised for his portrayal of the right-hand man to Mafia boss Tony Soprano. Van Zandt discussed his acting method. "I modeled the role on *The Sopranos* after my real role in life with Bruce. You'd see Silvio have to deliver bad news, Tony Soprano would get totally angry, and guess what? That's part of the job of being the *consigliere*, or being the best friend in real life. The main job of a producer is telling the artist the song's not good enough yet. You try to be as truthful as you can be without being insulting. And then you get past it."

The Boss and his first lieutenant: Bruce with "Miami" Steve Van Zandt, 1980.

BRUCE SPRINGSTEEN's rise to superstardom was a gradual one. Critical plaudits for his first two albums were followed by the breakthrough success of the *Born to Run* album and single in 1974. Famed for his marathon stage shows, he remains one of rock's must-see live performers.

"Bobby Jean" appears on 1984's *Born in the USA*, his seventh studio LP and the one that catapulted him into the major league, selling more than 15 million copies. Although Springsteen continued to tour with the E Street Band, *Born in the USA* was the last time the full line-up would work together on record for 18 years. Springsteen dismissed the band in 1989, although they got back together, Van Zandt included, briefly in 1995 and more permanently for a reunion tour in 1999.

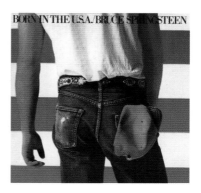

Carey
Joni Mitchell

Road trips have inspired some of Joni Mitchell's finest work. Time out from her "day job" has regularly allowed the introspective singer-songwriter to recharge her creative batteries and given her the time and space to reflect.

Travel animates her. In 2002 she released *Travelogue*, a double album of orchestral rearrangements of 22 of her songs. Three were from *Hejira*, her own favorite album from more than 40 years of recorded output. *Hejira*, which means "journey" in Arabic, was the product of a journey by car across America from Maine to California in the winter of 1976. *Blue*, the 1971 album that includes the song "Carey," was the result of another journey she made during 1970 on the hippie trail through Europe.

Its 1970 predecessor *Ladies of the Canyon* had been Mitchell's most successful release to date. *Canyon* included a hit single, "Big Yellow Taxi," and the folk anthems of her hippie generation, "Woodstock" and "The Circle Game." Joni was in huge demand, and responded by taking time out from performing to write, paint, and above all travel.

Her 1970 journey took her to the UK, France, and Spain, and eventually to Greece. She and her traveling companion, a poet called

The beach at Matala in southern Crete as it looked in 2011. The caves, now abandoned, are at the base of the cliff.

Penelope, met with hostility in Athens. As hippies, they stood out in a capital controlled at the time by a military junta. They escaped to the island of Crete, where despite the authorities' disapproval there was a flourishing hippie community at Matala on the south coast, brushed by warm winds from Africa. It was here that Joni met Carey.

Matala had been an established commune since beatniks discovered it in the 1950s. A handful of small buildings and fisherman's huts clustered around the water's edge on a small bay framed by two tall cliffs. The hippies themselves lived in a remarkable collection of natural and man-made caves in the cliffs, some dating back to the Bronze Age Minoan era.

They had been used at various times since then as a leper colony and as burial chambers—to Mitchell's horror she saw hippies wearing necklaces of human teeth. She recalls that she and Penelope looked decidedly unhip when she arrived, with dry-cleaning creases in their jeans. After a couple of days on the beach, however, they were accepted into the cave community.

The houses on the bay were occupied by Greeks and other nationals who made a living from the custom either of the hippies themselves or from the tourists who came to stare at them.

There were three shops and two restaurants. As Joni walked past one of them, the Delphini Café, a gas cooker exploded and the chef was thrown out through a window by the blast. The chef's dramatic exit immediately endeared him to the singer and they became firm friends. He was a stocky dropout from the University of North Carolina with a shock of (on that occasion literally) flaming red hair poking out from beneath a filthy off-white turban. This, combined with his surname, gave him the nickname Carrot Radish; his real name was Carey Raditz. He gave Joni a pair of his boots when her own unsuitable city shoes wore out on the local rocks; they shared a taste for Mickey Mouse chocolate bars and drove around Crete together in Joni's VW camper van; and for his birthday she wrote him the song "Carey."

The Delphini (Dolphin in English) became the Mermaid Café in the lyrics of "Carey." The song, which is as much about the tension between homesickness and carefree traveling as it is about Carey, holds many references to Mitchell's time in Greece among

> These freaks and these soldiers
> … beneath the Matala Moon

A sun-tanned Joni Mitchell performing at the Isle of Wight Festival in August 1970.

There is some debate about the "cane" in the line "Carey, get out your cane." Some suggest that it is cocaine, and that Mitchell also hints at the drug in the song "Coyote" on *Hejira* when she sings of "the fine white lines of the freeway." But Mitchell described Carey in 1971 as leaning on his cane. In 2010 a comment appeared online from someone claiming that a friend had met Joni and Carey at Matala and shared a bottle of wine at the Delphini; Carey then sprained his ankle in a drunken fall, and the unnamed friend gave him a cane to walk with.

This explanation seems to fit the mood of the song. It's an upbeat picture of relaxed times and joyous casual friendship, driven along by party handclaps and the strummed strings of an Appalachian dulcimer. Joni had taught herself to play the instrument, which was more portable than a guitar, on this European trip. Its jangly sound is the defining tone of the *Blue* album. The album includes the dulcimer-led song "California," which also refers to Carey, the "redneck on a Grecian isle … the red, red rogue who cooked good omelettes."

After Joni Mitchell's four months at Matala, she returned to gigging with renewed energy in July and, at the end of August, appeared at the first Isle of Wight Festival. She quickly introduced new songs (including "Carey") into her set that would be released on *Blue* the following June. Late in 1970 she appeared onstage with Frank Zappa at New York's legendary Fillmore East, when she read a new poem called "Penelope."

And what of Carey Raditz? After the cave dwellers of the Matala community were dispersed by the Greek police, he followed the hippie road to Nepal. In 1987 songwriter Eric Andersen, an old friend of Mitchell's, reported that Carey had gone back to college to finish his studies and was his roommate in New York. In a 1997 *Vanity Fair* interview Mitchell said Raditz was still in her life. After a spell in California, Carey now lives in Virginia; he is a certified financial planner, giving budgetary advice to NGO enterprises in Africa. By all accounts the wild days are behind him.

At this distance, memories of those far-off, hazy, happy, hippie days are a little unreliable. Many who claim they were there in Crete have different versions of events; even Joni Mitchell used to tell contradictory stories of their first meeting when she introduced the song onstage. The song itself is the best record we have of Joni's time in Matala and of her friend Carey:

> The bright red devil
> Who keeps me in this tourist town.

JONI MITCHELL, already the recipient of a Grammy for Best Folk Performance earned by her second album, *Clouds*, had David Crosby to lean on for advice while recording her third LP, *Ladies of the Canyon*. The songs she wrote during the months she took off to travel for her next album took her into another league entirely. Comparing Mitchell's talent to his own many years later, Crosby said, "By the time she did *Blue* she was past me and rushing toward the horizon."

In 2002 Mitchell received a Lifetime Achievement Grammy, not long after the *New York Times* had chosen *Blue* as one of the 25 albums that represented "turning points and pinnacles in 20th-century popular music."

Despite claiming to have retired from music in 2002, she released an album of new material, *Shine*, in 2007.

Cast No Shadow
Oasis

In December 1993, Manchester rock quintet Oasis were relatively unknown. Although recently signed by Creation Records, they were still doing support gigs. Famously arrogant, the band were contemptuous of some headliners like indie dance-popsters Saint Etienne. An invitation to open for fellow Lancastrians the Verve was, however, greeted with more enthusiasm. Here was a band that Oasis respected. Verve frontman Richard Ashcroft and Oasis's Noel Gallagher were kindred spirits.

The enigmatic and slightly cadaverous Richard Ashcroft of the Verve.

Ashcroft's childhood had been disrupted by the death of his father when he was 11. He fell under the influence of his stepfather, a member of the Rosicrucians, an ancient metaphysical secret society. This sparked an interest in transcendentalism, which led to him to be known for a time as "mad Richard" in the music press because of his claim that he could fly (he meant it in a purely musical sense).

Richard Ashcroft formed the Verve at college in his native Wigan in 1989. Their spacey, psychedelic sound transfixed audiences, and after three critically acclaimed singles the band unleashed their debut album, *A Storm in Heaven,* in 1993.

Two years later, Oasis were enjoying phenomenal sales of their second album *(What's the Story) Morning Glory?* Meanwhile, Ashcroft had broken up the Verve in September 1995, shortly after the release of *A Northern Soul,* a more conventional rock album. Noel Gallagher dedicated "Cast No Shadow" "to the genius of Richard Ashcroft" on *Morning Glory*'s sleeve notes. Noel explained the song's origins. "Richard wasn't very happy for a while so I wrote it for him and about three weeks later he quit the band. It's about songwriters in general who are desperately trying to say something."

> Bound with all the weight of all the words he tried to say
> As he faced the sun he cast no shadow

The influence and admiration was mutual. Oasis's megahit "Wonderwall" owed a little to the Verve's 1995 single "History," while Ashcroft dedicated the title track of *A Northern Soul* to Gallagher.

Ashcroft also paid tribute to his friend's importance. "Because of the nature of Oasis when they arrived, there was a big vacuum, everyone was scared of rock'n'roll. And Noel did it. Noel showed the way for a lot of people that there's still some great songs to be written."

The Verve reconvened in 1996 and went on to their period of greatest commercial success with the singles "Bittersweet Symphony," "The Drugs Don't Work," and "Lucky Man" from the era-defining *Urban Hymns* album. A second split followed in 1999 when Ashcroft went solo, but another reunion produced the album *Forth* in 2007. The Verve has been on hold since 2009 with Ashcroft now trading as RPA and the United Nations of Sound.

OASIS were driven by the turbulent relationship between brothers Liam and Noel Gallagher and this eventually caused the band to implode. The band's anthemic guitar rock helped usher in the Britpop era of the mid-Nineties. Their 1995 LP *(What's the Story) Morning Glory?* sold more than 15 million copies worldwide. They remained a massive live attraction, regularly filling stadiums around the world. The band's seventh and final album *Dig Out Your Soul* appeared in 2008. After a climactic argument between the brothers in 2009, Noel Gallagher left the band and Oasis were over. Liam now fronts Beady Eye.

A Day in the Life
The Beatles

Tara Browne was the epitome of swinging London in the 1960s. He was good looking, rich, knew the Beatles and the Stones, and was beginning to dabble in drugs. He was killed when his turquoise Lotus Elan went straight through a set of red stop lights and collided with a parked truck. Minutes before, witnesses estimated he was doing close to 100 mph on the Earls Court Road. He died in the hospital the next day.

Tara Browne was born into money and privilege. His father was Dominick Browne, the 4th Baron Oranmore and Browne, an Anglo-Irish aristocrat who would eventually sit in the House of Lords for a record 71 years, until ejected by Tony Blair's reforms. His mother had the money. She was Oonagh Guinness, youngest of the three "Golden Guinness Girls" and heiress to the brewing fortune. By the time her son was ripping up the streets of London in his fiberglass-bodied sportscar, she was on to her third husband.

The wrecked turquoise Lotus Elan of Guinness heir Tara Browne. The passenger in the front seat, model Suki Potier, managed to walk away from the crash.

Tara was sent to Britain's elite public school Eton, where he met many of the faces that would become part of London's hip '60s scene. He also met and befriended aspiring poet Hugo Williams who wrote about their time together in the *Spectator* magazine. "At 15, in 1960, Tara was barely literate, having walked out of dozens of schools. ... In his green suits, mauve shirts with amethyst cufflinks, his waves of blonde hair, brocade ties and buckled shoes, smoking

At 21, Browne was already married with two children and heading for divorce.

menthol cigarettes (always Salem), and drinking Bloody Marys, he was Little Lord Fauntleroy, Beau Brummell, Peter Pan, Terence Stamp in *Billy Budd*, David Hemmings in *Blow-Up*. His drawly Irish blarney was the perfect antidote to our public school reserve and what would come to be called 'postwar austerity.'"

After he left school, Browne's attention switched to the burgeoning scene in London. He got married to Noreen McSherry at 18, had two sons, Dorian and Julian, and opened a shop in the King's Road, the nexus of swinging London. While Hugo Williams was globe-trotting, compiling poems for his first publication, the Honourable Tara Browne (on the death of his father he would inherit the Baronetcy) was hanging out with John Paul Getty and becoming an established figure in London's hippest circles. When he met up with Williams again their paths were dividing.

"His money and youth made him a natural prey to certain charismatic Chelsea types who turned him into what he amiably termed a 'hustlee.' He reputedly gave Paul McCartney his first acid trip. The pair went to Liverpool together, got stoned, and cruised the city on mopeds until Paul went over the handlebars and broke a tooth and they had to call on Paul's Aunt Bett for assistance. There is still a body of people—and a book called *The Walrus Is Paul*—who believe that Paul is dead and is now actually Tara Browne with plastic surgery."

At the time of Browne's fatal accident on December 18, 1966, he was already estranged from his wife Noreen and going through a very high-profile custody battle in the High Court. In the passenger seat of the car was his new girlfriend, model Suki Potier. At the inquest for the accident, she maintained that Browne wasn't going fast and swerved to avoid an oncoming car. She escaped the accident unhurt. The inquest was published in the *Daily Mail* on January 17, 1967. Sitting at his piano composing songs, John Lennon read the news about his privileged acquaintance, "a lucky man who'd made the grade."

> He blew his mind out in a car
> He didn't notice that the lights had changed
> A crowd of people stood and stared
> They'd seen his face before
> Nobody was really sure
> If he was from the House of Lords

Browne's death proved to be the lyrical inspiration for half of what many consider to be the Beatles' finest song, closing their best album, *Sergeant Pepper*. The song itself was an amalgamation of two song halves; one was written by Lennon, the other by Paul McCartney, which producer George Martin melded together with an inspiring orchestral arrangement finishing on a grand E chord, symbolizing heaven.

THE BEATLES set the world alight, becoming the most recognizable foursome on the planet. "A Day in the Life" was the final track on *Sgt. Pepper's Lonely Hearts Club Band*—often voted as the greatest album of all time. "A Day in the Life" was never released as a single but, like many other tracks, became embedded in public consciousness. The album continued to sweep up awards in the years after its 1967 release. *Sgt. Pepper* went 11 times platinum in the U.S., bettered only by later releases *The Beatles* and *Abbey Road*.

A psychedelic Buick with Tara Browne center back. The front row is the team of Binder, Edwards, and Vaughan (BEV), who created the psychedelic frontage of Browne's King's Road boutique, Dandie Fashions, and produced psychedelic art on Browne's AC Cobra and Paul McCartney's piano. The car would later be used on the cover of the Kinks' single "Sunny Afternoon."

Diamonds and Rust
Joan Baez

Back in the early 1960s, Joan Baez was the Queen of Folk Music. Her 1960 debut album *Joan Baez* had stayed on the Billboard chart for two years and was joined in 1962 by *Joan Baez Vol 2*, which went gold. They in turn were followed by *Joan Baez Live In Concert, Part 1* and *Part 2*, both also going gold. Her domination of the folk scene in the United States was complete.

Baez embraced the ethos of the American folk music revival begun by Pete Seeger, Woody Guthrie, and their peers in the 1940s. In a time before pop, "popular music" meant "music of the people," music of ordinary folk—folk music. The folk revival used the traditional songs of ordinary people to give them a voice in important political issues of the day such as Vietnam and the H-bomb.

At a civil rights rally in Washington, DC, in August 1963 Baez shared a stage with Bob Dylan and other leading folk artists singing the protest standard "We Shall Overcome." It was the same occasion at which Martin Luther King Jr. gave his world-changing speech "I have a dream." Baez and Dylan had first sung together in public earlier in the year; they performed one of Dylan's compositions, "With God On Our Side," first at the Monterey Jazz Festival and then at the Newport Folk Festival (where Baez had made her debut in 1959).

Bob Dylan arrived in New York in January 1961 and began to make a name for himself in the folk clubs of the city's Greenwich Village district. Baez was unimpressed when she first saw the newcomer that year. Indeed, his first album *Bob Dylan* released in 1962 sold only 5,000 copies, barely enough to cover its costs. But by the time she introduced him at Monterey he had matured immeasurably as a writer and singer. His new album, *The Freewheelin' Bob Dylan*, included the song which would become a new protest classic, "Blowin' in the Wind." Dylan had found his voice.

Joan admired the direct political stance of Dylan's songs and gave the emerging young protest singer-songwriter valuable exposure by regularly inviting him to join her onstage. That admiration turned to mutual attraction over the summer of 1963 and they began an onstage and offstage relationship that continued for two years.

Bob Dylan and Joan Baez, photographed shortly after arriving in London, April 26, 1965. He was the headline act on their European tour, and she was the support.

> Well you burst on the scene, already a legend
> The unwashed phenomenon, the original vagabond

Although Joan and Bob were born within five months of each other in 1941, they represented quite different musical traditions. This became apparent at the 1965 Newport Festival when, to the shock and horror of his folk audience, Dylan was backed by electric rock musicians. It is impossible to overstate the impact of that performance—it changed folk music forever, paving the way for the folk-rock of the Byrds, Joni Mitchell, and all who followed in their wake. At Newport, Dylan the iconoclast was making it clear that he would not be constrained by any conventional wisdom about the definition of folk music.

Perhaps he saw Baez as representing that convention. Dylan began to distance himself from her; he ignored Baez in public, and in private (according to their friends) he spoke aggressively and critically to her. She recalls that betrayal of trust in the song "Diamonds and Rust":

> My poetry was lousy, you said
> Where are you calling from?

Dylan was now the star and Baez the support act; on an English tour in 1965, she was hurt that he never invited her to join him onstage. Although her career was on the wane at that point, she had hoped for some acknowledgment of the boost she had given him in the same manner two years earlier.

Joan left the tour and returned early to America. When she visited Bob's house and found Sara Lowndes there, she knew at last that their relationship was over. It emerged that Dylan and Lowndes (a friend of his manager's daughter) had been having an affair since 1964, and they were married in November 1965.

Baez was heartbroken but recognized the important change that Dylan's genius was bringing to folk music. In 1968 she released *Any Day Now*, an entire album of Dylan covers. By 1972 she had enough distance from the affair to write the song "To Bobby," urging him to remain politically active. Then in 1975, nearly a decade after the romance had died, a rare phone call from Dylan to Baez triggered all her bittersweet memories of the relationship to painfully and lucidly return.

> It's all come back too clearly
> Yes I loved you dearly
> And if you're offering me diamonds and rust
> I've already paid

He rang her from a phone booth in the Midwest to read some new lyrics to her, perhaps missing the rapport they used to share as fellow musicians. (Lowndes was an actress and sometime *Playboy* Bunny.) Baez told him he was just being nostalgic, and if not,

Then give me another word for it,
You who are so good with words
And at keeping things vague

She wrote about the diamonds and the rust, the good and bad memories that follow any failed relationship. Dylan's with Sara was itself failing, and Joan may have drawn some satisfaction from the end of that union in 1977; but her own brief marriage, in 1967 to antidraft activist David Harris, had already collapsed in 1973.

Although critical of Dylan's nostalgia, Joan nevertheless agreed to join his legendary Rolling Thunder Revue in 1975–76, singing several duets with him. There have been occasional reunions since—a Peace Concert in 1980 and another painful tour in 1984, in which Baez found herself not duetting with Dylan as promised but merely opening for him.

Although their romantic involvement ended almost 50 years ago, Dylan and Baez remain forever bound together in the public eye as king and queen of their separate but overlapping folk traditions. Baez's 1987 memoirs were vitriolic about Dylan, but his own in 2005 were warm. "The sight of her made me sigh," he wrote. "All that, and then there was the voice. She sang in a voice straight to God."

JOAN BAEZ was a talented songwriter, as "Diamonds and Rust" proved, but it was her preference for playing other artists' material that would ultimately hold her back. Her eighth album, 1968's *Joan*, had been a selection of contemporary pop songs, signaling a change in direction from strictly traditional folk fare. Throughout the 1980s and 1990s, Baez continued to protest for civil rights, equality, and nonviolence and was involved in 1985's Live Aid concerts, opening the US segment. In 2007 she finally picked up a Grammy for Lifetime Achievement after missing out during her career, despite six nominations.

Do You Really Want to Hurt Me

Culture Club

Had it been up to Boy George, Culture Club's breakthrough hit would not have seen the light of day. "Our first two singles failed," he explained. "That single was our last chance. But I threatened to leave if [the label] released it. I didn't think it was us; it wasn't club music. It wouldn't stand up to Spandau Ballet. But I was wrong."

George had an ulterior motive for resisting the release of "Do You Really Want To Hurt Me." The lyrics were a portrait of his stormy love affair with the band's drummer Jon Moss. "It was so personal in a way that our other songs weren't. It was about Jon. All the songs were about him, but they were more ambiguous."

> Precious kisses
> Words that burn me

London-born Moss had played with punk band the Damned, replacing original drummer Rat Scabies for a while in 1978, and then working briefly with Adam and the Ants before receiving the call from Boy George to join his new group. Moss came up with the name Culture Club, an allusion to the differing ethnic backgrounds of the four members—"an Irish transvestite, a Jew, a black man and an Anglo-Saxon." Moss also maintains that he and his bandmates persuaded George to adopt the prefix Boy, rather than Papa.

Because the first two singles "White Boy" and "I'm Afraid of Me" made no impact on the charts, morale in the ranks was low when they ventured into the BBC studios to record a Radio 1 session for DJ Peter Powell's show in 1982. They found themselves with some spare studio time after they had recorded their contribution, and the loping groove of "Do You Really Want to Hurt Me" was born during a loose jam.

Musical perfection and mass acceptance came together in four minutes and 25 seconds of white soul vocals, spacey reggae bass, understated yet insistent drumming, and chiming guitar. As it turned out, "Hurt Me" would top the UK chart and become the first of half a dozen Top Ten hits for Culture Club in the United States. Having overcome his initial feeling that "it was too personal and wasn't a dance record," George conceded that it was "a really well constructed song. It's probably the only proper song we've got with proper chord changes and keyboard changes in it. It's just very musical."

He believed that its universal appeal lay in the fact that "the most powerful songs are love songs. They apply to everyone—especially kids who fall in and out of love more times than anyone else. At the end of the day, everybody wants to be wanted." Credited to all four members of the band, "Do You Really Want to Hurt Me" would appear on their debut album *Kissing to Be Clever*. The single made an international star of the former George O'Dowd, who was instantly recognizable because of his androgynous appearance and uniquely eclectic sense of style.

Boy George and Jon Moss in Tokyo, August 1985.

Although Moss was heterosexual, he and George quickly became lovers, keeping their affair secret from not only the press and public but from the rest of the band as well. Their relationship was volatile and sometimes violent. The end of their liaison precipitated the end of Culture Club.

Shortly after the split, George showed remorse over talking in public about Moss. "Jon was somebody I really loved and I've said things about him that I've really regretted. I'm really sorry about all the bad things I said about him. I did mean them but I should have just said them to him."

The publication of George's autobiography *Take It Like a Man* in 1995 reignited the war of words. Moss denied his former lover's claim that he was embarrassed by the relationship.

"I'm not ashamed of anything. My parents know, all my friends knew. There's no problem there." He added that "the only person George loves is George. ... He's like a nightmare ex-wife." The singer's refusal to take part in Culture Club's 2006 reunion tour caused further recriminations.

Moss subsequently married and is the father of three children. His post–Culture Club musical projects included the group Promised Land and drumming on the charity single "People I Don't Know Are Trying to Kill Me" in aid of the victims of the London bombings in July 2005.

George's attention was initially focused on overcoming a drug habit. This achieved, for a time at least, his solo career started brightly in 1987 with the UK chart-topping "Everything I Own." The 1990s saw him diversify into DJing, writing books, designing clothes, and taking photos, while a stage show of his life, *Taboo*, enjoyed success in London's West End in 2002. When it transferred to Broadway, however, it was savaged by the critics and he sunk back into drug use.

A 2006 TV documentary saw him allow cameras into his east London flat, which was decorated with homoerotic artworks. Reminiscent of Tracey Emin, his bed linen was decorated with the names of people he had slept with, including Jon Moss.

CULTURE CLUB was assembled by Boy George, a face in the New Romantic London scene of the early 1980s. He recruited Jon Moss, plus guitarist and keyboardist Roy Hay and bass player Mikey Craig. In October 1982, "Do You Really Want to Hurt Me" topped the charts in the UK and then all over the world, peaking at #2 in the US. Their debut album *Kissing to Be Clever* spawned two further international hits and the follow-up *Colour by Numbers* included another UK #1 in "Karma Chameleon." After less-successful follow-up albums, Culture Club eventually disbanded in 1986. The original line-up reformed between 1998 and 2002 for another album, *Don't Mind If I Do*, and two more British hit singles.

Moss and George enjoy an intimate moment backstage before the 1984 San Remo Music Festival in Italy. After they fell out, Moss described George as "a nightmare ex-wife."

George's private life hit the headlines again when he spent a spell sweeping the streets of New York after a cocaine bust, and in 2009 he served four months of a 15-month prison sentence for falsely imprisoning a male escort. An attempt to relaunch his career via a spell on TV's *Celebrity Big Brother* proved impossible under the terms of his early release.

In 2010, Boy George and Moss's relationship was depicted in a British TV drama, *Worried About the Boy*. The singer acted as a consultant on the project, lending some of his outfits and sending 17-year-old Douglas Booth, who played him, a friendly message. "George sent me a message before we started filming, saying, 'I just want to wish you the best of luck … and don't be camp!' He didn't want anyone to play him as a camp stereotype, because actually he's quite manly." Yet that same year found the singer once more expressing regret over his compulsion to air his feelings in public, particularly his relationship with Jon. "I've learned the hard way that some things are private."

Hey Jude
The Beatles

"Hey Jude" was released in 1968 and was the first Beatles track to be released on their own record label, Apple. It would go on to become one of their most anthemic tracks and, while over seven minutes long, would nevertheless become an airplay classic.

The song remained close to the hearts of the Fab Four's songwriting team of John Lennon and Paul McCartney. McCartney wrote the song for John's five-year-old son Julian Lennon to comfort him while his father and estranged wife Cynthia were enduring an acrimonious divorce in the wake of Lennon's infidelity.

The separation came after a tempestuous decade-long relationship that began before the Beatles hit international stardom. Cynthia was just 19 when she met John at college and immediately took a dislike to him. "He was scruffy, dangerous-looking and totally disruptive. He frightened the life out of me," she later recalled. But what originally offended her eventually attracted her to Lennon, and before she knew it, she was married with a child on the way.

Julian would be born into the mad global roadshow that was Beatlemania, just as it was kicking off in April 1963. In what would serve as a symbolic precursor for the majority of their relationship, John didn't see Julian for the first time until he was three days old. Julian would eventually become almost the forgotten son and would never enjoy the relationship with his father that his half-brother, Sean, would.

Lennon and Cynthia would split after his affair with Japanese artist Yoko Ono, and Julian would have minimal contact with him in the immediate years after the divorce.

Julian Lennon with Paul McCartney and Jane Asher arriving back from India.

McCartney, who originally penned the song as "Hey Jules" during the divorce, would become very close to Julian, and would go on to become something of an uncle figure to him as he grew up. Julian Lennon himself later said: "We had a great friendship going and there seems to be far more pictures of me and Paul playing together at that age than there are pictures of me and my dad."

"Hey Jude" was penned in its earliest incarnation while McCartney was visiting Cynthia and John's Surrey mansion just after Lennon's wife had discovered that he was having an affair. Eager to help, McCartney wrote a song intended to comfort the youngster in the midst of a breakup that would not end favorably for either him or his mother; Cynthia would receive a settlement of just £150,000, while Julian would be sent a paltry £100 a week in maintenance. Although the song would later become "Hey Jude," as McCartney believed this was easier to sing, the sentiment remained.

Years later Paul would reveal the origins of the song, with Julian recalling: "Paul told me he'd been thinking about my circumstances, about what I was going through and what I'd have to go through. ... It surprises me whenever I hear the song. It's strange to think someone has written a song about you. It still touches me."

THE BEATLES' "Hey Jude" would become arguably the most successful track the group would ever release, hitting #1 in both the US and UK, breaking radio conventions in the process; all seven minutes were broadcast at a time when most tracks were generally less than half that length. It was released as a single in August 1968 but did not appear on an album until February 1970. It was included on *Hey Jude* (a compilation of singles that up until then had not appeared on an album in the US). In the UK, it was not included on an album until the *1967–1970* compilation (also known as the *Blue Album*) in 1973.

How Do You Sleep?

John Lennon

Not all the players at the recording session for "How Do You Sleep?", a track on John Lennon's *Imagine* album, may have been fully aware of the meaning behind the lyrics. But it was obvious to Ringo Starr when he walked in. He immediately said, "That's enough, John."

The session featured many musicians with a connection to Lennon's old group, the Beatles. Klaus Voorman on bass had been a friend since the band's early days in Hamburg and had designed the cover for their *Revolver* album. On drums was Alan White, a relative tyro who had learned to play by copying Beatles drummer Ringo's style before being invited to join the Plastic Ono Band by John and Yoko in 1969. Nicky Hopkins on electric piano had been a session keyboard player on many Beatles tracks including "Revolution." Fellow Beatle George Harrison gave "How Do You Sleep?" its defining guitar part.

Notably absent from this band of Fab Four alumni was Lennon's former writing partner Paul McCartney. Although all four Beatles released solo projects before the breakup, John blamed Paul for the group's final disintegration in 1971. "How Do You Sleep?" was his bitter and vicious swipe at McCartney.

Almost every line of the song is a harsh attack on his boyhood friend, the influence of McCartney's partner Linda ("Jump when your mama tell you anything") and his entourage ("The straights who tell you you was king"). One of the saddest couplets belittles Paul's contribution to the Beatles as a composer of "muzak." Fans have long been split between Lennon, with his songwriting debt to the gritty roots of rock'n'roll, and McCartney, who adhered to a more melodic pop tradition.

Lennon and McCartney in 1968 on their way to launch Apple in New York.

> The only thing you did was Yesterday
> And since you're gone you're just Another Day

Elsewhere in the song Lennon makes bitter references to Paul's reputation as the best-looking member of the band—"a pretty face may last a year or two"—and to the rumors around the time of the *Abbey Road* album that Paul had died—"Those freaks was right when they said you was dead." (See "A Day in the Life," page 28.)

With no reconciliation, fans interpreted many songs from their solo outputs as further salvoes in the musical set-to started by "How Do You Sleep?" Paul's perennial live favorite "Let Me Roll It" (see page 60) from his album *Band on the Run* was considered an early riposte.

The pair were eventually able to patch things up, although the friendship never returned to its former intimacy. The last time Paul and John met face-to-face was several years before Lennon's assassination in 1980. Only four days before his death John Lennon discussed the song in a BBC radio interview. "It was creative rivalry," he said. "It was not a vicious vendetta … but I felt resentment, so I used that situation … to write 'How Do You Sleep?'" In a *Times* interview in 2008 Paul remarked, "The answer to John was … I was sleeping very well."

JOHN LENNON was murdered at the age of 40 ensuring that he, like Holly and Hendrix, would become a rock icon. Lennon fans enjoyed six solo albums before his 1980 posthumous comeback with *Double Fantasy,* an album that reflected his happiness at being a husband and father to second son Sean.

"How Do You Sleep?" appeared on the 1971 release *Imagine.* His songwriting, initially soured by the Beatles split, would later become secondary to his politics and the battle to remain a US resident. He had moved to New York City in 1971, and his open criticism of the Vietnam War led Richard Nixon's administration to attempt to deport him.

Hurdy Gurdy Man
Donovan

"Hurdy Gurdy Man" was a big hit for Scots-born singer-songwriter Donovan Leitch in the summer of 1968, reaching #4 in the UK and #5 in the US. Donovan would later say the song was inspired by a vision he experienced in Hawaii watching the surf break on the rocks, during which he encountered a man floating above the waves playing a hurdy-gurdy.

A hurdy-gurdy is a stringed instrument of medieval origin on which the strings are rubbed by a rosined wheel that functions like a violin bow. The wheel is turned by the player's right hand while the left plays the music on the keys in the key box. The resultant sound is actually more like bagpipes or a barrel organ than strings.

The song was written in Donovan's cottage in Hertfordshire following his visit to India in February 1968. He had been invited to Rishikesh on

At the ashram in Rishikesh: (L–R) John Lennon, Paul McCartney, Maharishi Mahesh Yogi, George Harrison, Mia Farrow, Johnny Farrow, and Donovan.

the banks of the Ganges to study under the Maharishi Mahesh Yogi, a well-known advocate for world peace and the person responsible for developing the technique known as Transcendental Meditation (TM), which would subsequently be taken up by hundreds of thousands of Westerners.

The entourage comprised Beatles John, Paul, George, and Ringo, plus wives and friends that included Cynthia Lennon, Pattie Boyd, and Jane Asher. In India the party was joined by other celebrities including actress Mia Farrow and Beach Boy Mike Love.

The Beatles had met with the Maharishi the previous year in London and then in Bangor, North Wales, and it has been said that he helped wean the Fab Four off LSD. Indeed, following their experiences with TM and that stay in India, the Beatles entered arguably their most creative period, writing almost all the material for both *The Beatles* (aka the *White Album*) and *Abbey Road*.

The time spent in India was creatively fertile for Donovan, too, who spent days hanging out playing music, particularly with McCartney and Harrison. George was given many instruments during his stay and one of these, a tambura, he gave as a gift to Donovan. "I picked it up," recalled Donovan in his 2005 autobiography, "and realized that this four-string gourd was about as much I could muster. I began to make a tune of my own which related very closely to the 'airs' of my Celtic past and what I played would later evolve into my song 'Hurdy Gurdy Man.'"

The Hurdy Gurdy Man to whom the title refers is Donovan's old guitar teacher and friend Mac MacLeod, whom Don had first met on the Hertfordshire folk scene back in the early 1960s, notably at The Cock pub in St. Albans. Mac had taught Donovan a number of styles, such as Travis picking; he'd later play with him at the *New Musical Express* Poll Winners' Concert at Wembley in early 1965 and go on national tour with him on the back of Donovan's first big hit "Catch the Wind."

But as Donovan's star had been rising internationally with a string of hit singles on both sides of the Atlantic, Mac disappeared off to Scandinavia to pursue other musical directions. Mac and his two fellow musicians in the band, drummer Jens Otzen and guitarist Claus Bohling were swept up in the spirit of the era and decided to form a psychedelic power trio in the style of Cream and the Jimi Hendrix Experience. They called themselves Hurdy Gurdy.

As 1967's Summer of Love wore on, Hurdy Gurdy became one of Copenhagen's biggest acts, playing a two-week residency at the concert hall in the Tivoli and breaking all previous attendance records. The band was hot, and record labels wanted to sign them, but then Mac was jailed for possessing a quantity of hash. He wrote to Donovan's then manager Ash Kozack from his Danish prison cell, explaining his predicament and saying that once he had disentangled himself, he intended to bring the band to England—could Donovan help?

Hurdy Gurdy turned up at Donovan's cottage in Little Berkhamsted, set up, and played the song Donovan had started writing on George Harrison's gifted tambura on his lawn. Their long improvisations, changing rhythms, and moods and textures were not what Donovan was expecting—they were far too heavy for his delicate song.

He decided to keep the number for himself, telling the *NME* that "Hurdy Gurdy Man" was "originally written for a Danish band by that name. There is a friend of mine in that group, Mac MacLeod, whom I looked to in the early days to learn how to pick guitar. I wrote the song especially for them—but then we got into a disagreement over how it was to be produced. I wanted to do it one way, and they another. So I said 'Right then, I'll do it myself' because I think it's good enough to be a hit. So I've done it."

Donovan took the song into the studio and recorded it under the direction of his regular producer Mickie Most and engineer Eddie Kramer.

DONOVAN LEITCH came to prominence in the era of peace and love. The hippie singer-songwriter was discovered while busking before recording a demo and being signed to a record label. Donovan gained fame in the US in 1966 with his chart-topping "Sunshine Superman." "Hurdy Gurdy Man" has been recorded by a wide variety of acts, including singer Eartha Kitt, hippie guitarist Steve Hillage, and alternative American rockers the Butthole Surfers, whose version graced the soundtrack to the 1994 movie *Dumb and Dumber*. It has also been used in a number of other films, including David Fincher's *Zodiac* and Barry Levinson's *Sleepers*.

Donovan singing outside his cottage in rural Hertfordshire, where he would later audition Mac MacLeod's band, Hurdy Gurdy.

It was rumored that Jimmy Page played lead guitar on the song, while Led Zeppelin colleague-to-be John Paul Jones played bass and did the arrangement. Jeff Beck did actually lay down a lead but this was wiped from the mix.

For Donovan the sound of "Hurdy Gurdy Man" was quite a departure after his forays into folk, jazz, and Jamaican music on previous hits. After the warm acoustic opening, the song is dominated by crashing drums and "blazing rock fuzz-guitars." The droning sound many thought at the time was a hurdy-gurdy was in fact Donovan, sitting cross-legged on the studio floor, playing the tambura Harrison had given him in India.

George Harrison actually wrote a final verse for the song but it was not recorded at the time. As Donovan points out in his autobiography, "singles in those days were rarely longer than three minutes. The exciting power chord riff solos ... were too good to be cut short, so George's verse was left out." But it was finally recorded and released as part of Donovan's 1990 set, *The Classics Live,* and at shows, the singer is apt to tell the audience that Harrison's contribution tells of how the philosophies and teachings of the Maharishi were eventually rediscovered after a long period of centuries, suggesting that the Yogi himself might even have been the titular Hurdy Gurdy Man.

I Will Always Love You

Dolly Parton

Dolly Parton, the enormously successful singer from Sevierville, Tennessee, has earned her title as the Queen of Country Music. Her business interests alone make her one of the wealthiest women in the industry through her Dollywood theme park and the production company Sandollar, of which she is a partner. Sandollar is behind ventures such as TV's *Buffy the Vampire Slayer* and the film remakes *Father of the Bride* and *Sabrina*. As a performer, the most conservative estimates put her global sales at well over 150 million units.

She is the embodiment of the rags to riches story. Dolly Parton was born into a one-room shack as one of 12 children of what she calls a dirt-poor family. Her vocal talent was spotted from the beginning, and by the age of nine she was appearing on local Tennessee radio and TV stations. She first appeared at country music's shrine, the Grand Ole Opry in Nashville, when she was 13 years old.

She began writing songs with her uncle Bill Owens, and the chart success of their compositions for other country singers led to her first album, *Hello, I'm Dolly*, and first country hit as a performer, 1966's "Dumb Blonde." These in turn drew her to the attention of Porter Wagoner, host of a long-running and popular syndicated TV show.

Wagoner, a country music star since 1951, launched *The Porter Wagoner Show* in 1960. In 1967 his regular female vocalist Norma Jean was leaving after seven years to start a family and a solo career, buoyed by recent chart successes resulting from her TV exposure. Wagoner took Dolly Parton on as Norma Jean's replacement not only on screen but also in his live touring revue. And, as he had done for Norma Jean, he persuaded his record company RCA to sign Dolly too.

It was a tremendous opportunity for Dolly, although Porter's audience was not so sure. Norma Jean had been a fixture for seven years and was well liked by the program's viewers (which at its peak reached some three million). They found it hard to accept Dolly, going so far as to chant Norma Jean's name during performances.

Porter stood by his choice and introduced a new regular feature in the program in which he sang a duet with Dolly—something he had never done with her predecessor. The gimmick paid off, endearing Dolly to the TV audience and ensuring that the Wagoner-Parton duets became a fixture of the country charts throughout Dolly's time on the show. Dolly's solo career was initially much less successful, but in 1971 she had her first solo US Billboard Hot Country #1 with "Joshua."

From then on her star rose and soon eclipsed that of her mentor and benefactor Wagoner. She began to have ambitions beyond the small-town America venues she was limited to playing with Wagoner—his stage revue only toured to the rural areas to which *The Porter Wagoner Show* was syndicated. By 1974 she had equalled Norma Jean's seven years with the show and, buoyed by her solo chart success just as her predecessor had been, wanted to strike out on her own.

In 1973 she expressed her growing awareness that she needed to move on in her composition "I Will Always Love You."

> If I should stay
> Well I would only be in your way
> And so I'll go

She was overshadowing Porter, and her contract with him was certainly restricting her. But it was a binding one and eventually she had to buy her way out of it. She left the show in mid-1974, although she continued to record duets with Wagoner until 1975, and he continued to produce her solo recordings for another year after that.

"I Will Always Love You" is often described as a lament for the end of a romantic relationship, but Wagoner and Parton were never more than friendly colleagues—Parton married her husband Carl Dean the year before she joined the show and in 2011 they celebrated their 45th wedding anniversary.

The song is sometimes cited as evidence of rancor

An under-tressed Dolly Parton singing with Porter Wagoner in the late 1960s.

Back together again onstage at the Grand Ole Opry, Nashville, in 1978. Dolly's career—and her hairstyle—blossomed in the intervening years.

between Dolly and Porter surrounding her departure from the TV series. Although it is easy to imagine that Wagoner would not want her to leave—she must have been a great asset to the show's ratings—there is no evidence of a personal split between them. In fact, when Parton sang the song on the show in 1974, Wagoner introduced it with great warmth as "one of the most beautiful ballads that Miss Dolly has written."

Unlike Norma Jean, who never managed to recapture the success of her Wagoner years, Dolly flourished without the constraints of her contract with Porter. The song went on to become her second US Billboard Hot Country #1 of 1974, following the crossover hit "Jolene." It was recorded by many artists, although not by Elvis Presley, who intended to but wanted to be given half the composing royalties for the privilege. Dolly politely declined.

Instead, it was Linda Ronstadt's 1975 version that, in 1992, actor Kevin Costner brought to the attention of Whitney Houston, his costar in the film *The Bodyguard*. Houston needed a big ballad for her role, and her take on Dolly's simple country song, with the addition of a bold acappella introduction, became a worldwide hit. Houston's showcase version set records for sales and chart success not surpassed until Elton John's reworking of "Candle in the Wind" in 1997.

Porter Wagoner, about whom the song had originally been written, hosted his TV show until 1981. In 2002 Dolly inducted Porter into the Country Music Hall of Fame and in 2007 she performed at an event to celebrate his 50 years of membership of the Grand Ole Opry.

That year, two months before his 80th birthday, he released his last album, *Wagonmaster*, and opened for the White Stripes at Madison Square Gardens in New York. He died in October 2007. In April 2008 Dolly Parton performed a private memorial concert for his family and friends at Dollywood. The front row was completely taken up by Porter's family, the second by country music legends from the Grand Ole Opry. There wasn't a dry eye in the house when she closed proceedings, inevitably, with the song she had written for him 35 years earlier.

DOLLY PARTON wrote her first song at the age of five, and has since become the most successful female country performer of all time, having placed a record-breaking 26 country chart-topping singles and 42 Top Ten albums on the Billboard country charts. Almost all of her hits have been self-penned. "It was a song that brought me out of Smokey Mountains, and it was a song that took me all around the world ... even my theme park and my other business things all started with a song. It's been my songs that financed a lot of stuff until they stood on their own."

Hits range from US pop chart-topper "9 to 5" to her signature song "Jolene" to "I Will Always Love You," a song she's particularly proud of writing. "I am just grateful to Whitney Houston because she did a spectacular job on that. I have many awards and I'm very grateful for them all, but I think probably the things that mean the most to me are the things I win for songwriting."

Jeremy
Pearl Jam

irvana guitarist and singer Kurt Cobain, the figurehead of the grunge movement, stunned the world in 1994 by taking his own life with a shotgun. In contrast to the headlines he made worldwide, reports were somewhat less widespread when, three years earlier, a 15-year-old youth from the small US town of Richardsville, Texas, took the same way out after experiencing similar feelings of hopelessness and depression. In front of classmates who had been bullying him for the past few months, Jeremy Wade

A school photo of troubled teenager Jeremy Wade Delle.

Delle put the barrel of a .347 Magnum pistol into his mouth and pulled the trigger.

The story of Delle's suicide on January 8, 1991, touched a nerve in Eddie Vedder, lead singer of Seattle band and Nirvana rivals Pearl Jam. "Jeremy," a track from the quintet's 1991 debut album, *Ten*, told Delle's sad story and, after it became their third single, went on to sell well over a million copies.

"That kind of thing probably happens once a week in America," observed Vedder. "It's a by-product of the American fascination, or rather perversion, with guns. Parental neglect and abuse is the source of many problems. Childhood is such a critical time of a child's development. Many of the things that happen to you as a child resurface in later life."

Vedder's concern for and empathy with Jeremy may well reflect his own personality. Pearl Jam would go on to become one of the world's most successful rock acts, but as their fame spread, Vedder chose to withdraw into a cocoon of his own making. Rarely interviewed, the increasingly sensitive frontman shunned the spotlight, maintaining that his band's music expressed everything that they have to say. Whether this was due to insecurity or to a more fundamental dislike of the media is unclear. Vedder went on record expressing his sympathy for yet another American youth who was unable to find a place for himself in an increasingly complex society.

"Don't get me wrong, I wouldn't want to do it myself or anything," mused the man behind the lyrics, "but there's a sense of—and I frighten myself by relating to it so much—a sense of 'Fuck it, if I'm going down, and it's not my fault and I did everything I fucking could, and I worked with these hands and I didn't do drugs, if I'm out of here, then I'm taking a few people with me.'" These feelings of anger and despair are best summed up when Vedder croons:

> Picking on the boy
> Seemed a harmless little fuck
> But we unleashed a lion

"Jeremy" earned Pearl Jam a gold disc and set them on the path to worldwide superstardom—in 1992 they even managed to outsell Nirvana. The song scooped no less than four prizes at the MTV Awards, where Eddie Vedder revealed to the astonished crowd: "If it weren't for music, I'd have shot myself."

PEARL JAM developed from Seattle band Mother Love Bone and consisted of Eddie Vedder (vocals), Stone Gossard (guitar), Mike McCready (guitar), Jeff Ament (bass), and Dave Abbruzzese (drums). "Jeremy," one of their first singles, was taken from debut album *Ten* which, by late 1992, had reached #2 on the Billboard chart. By June 2011, it had sold 9,869,000 copies and remains their most commercially successful album.

They celebrated their 20th anniversary as a band in 2011. While few would have predicted their longevity, it was an example of how, as one blogger put it, the band had "maintained a rabid fanbase throughout two decades of running away from superstardom."

The Killing of Georgie (Part I & II)

Rod Stewart

In 1976 Rod Stewart was in the midst of the transition from bad-boy rocker to international superstar. Swedish actress Britt Ekland was the first of several high-profile girlfriends. She added some breathy French vocals to his single "Tonight's the Night," a song about loss of virginity, featuring lyrics considered too sexually explicit for some American radio stations. For the follow-up, Stewart chose another ballad, one with the potential for even more controversy. "The Killing of Georgie (Part I & II),"

"An ambulance screamed to a halt on 53rd and 3rd / Georgie's life ended there."

like several of Rod's songs, was based on real-life events, in this case the murder of a gay friend.

The identity of Georgie remained a matter of speculation until 1996 when Stewart revealed that it "was a true story about a gay friend of the Faces. He was especially close to me and Mac (Ian McLagan, Faces keyboardist). But he was shot or knifed, I can't remember which. That was a song I wrote totally on me own over the chord of open E."

The opening line refers to "changing ways" and "so-called liberated days" before boldly introducing the main character as "gay I guess … nothin' more or nothin' less." He was "the kindest guy I ever knew."

Georgie escapes small-town bigotry, including that of his own father—"how can my son not be straight?"—by fleeing to New York where he becomes the darling of the theatrical community.

The fatal attack comes when he is walking home from a show hand in hand with his boyfriend, although it is not clear whether the assault is motivated by that. The "New Jersey gang with just one aim" leave their victim with "a head hit (on) a sidewalk cornerstone."

Reflecting on the implications for his career, Stewart said, "I think it was a brave step, but it wasn't a risk. You can't write a song like that unless you've experienced it. But it was a subject that no one had approached before." Cynics may point out that a little controversy is a good way to sell records and the song provoked a mixed reaction from gay and heterosexual listeners.

"The Killing of Georgie" was responsible for launching some unlikely rumors that Stewart himself might be gay. As for how he came to write it, Rod speculated that, "It's probably because I was surrounded by gay people at that stage. I had a gay PR man, a gay manager. Everyone around me was gay." Even his best friend Elton.

At six and a half minutes, the song consisted of two distinct sections —part I recounts the story, part II is a lament for Georgie—which could be easily edited by radio programmers worried about its length, assuming they would play it in the first place.

During the sessions for his next album, 1977's *Footloose and Fancy Free*, Stewart recorded a sequel, "Innocent (The Killing of Georgie, Part III)" that concerns the gang member accused of Georgie's murder. This remained unreleased until 2009 when it finally saw the light of day as part of a boxed set *The Rod Stewart Sessions 1971–1998*, a collection of outtakes.

ROD STEWART, a former gravedigger, soccer player, and busker, had been making records in various guises since the mid-1960s. His moment arrived in 1971 when the single "Maggie May" and *Every Picture Tells a Story*, his third solo album, topped both the singles and album charts on both sides of the Atlantic. Stewart enjoyed a parallel career as lead singer of the Faces, a band notorious for their love of the rock'n'roll lifestyle. When the Faces split in 1975, Stewart relocated to America. "The Killing of Georgie" continued his run of Top Ten singles in Britain, reaching #2. Since the millennium he has been concentrating on reinterpretations of standards including five volumes of *The Great American Songbook*.

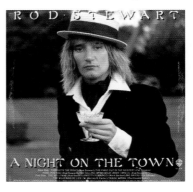

Kooks
David Bowie

Angie and David Bowie didn't have the average rock 'n' roll partnership. They met in London in 1969 while she was studying art at Kingston Polytechnic and he was an aspiring rock star. Bowie was on the rebound from the love of his life, Hermione Farthingale, who'd left their band Feathers to pursue a dancing career, leaving him to follow his dream of pop stardom after the brief success of his single "Space Odyssey." Angie's impact on his style and attitude was profound, encouraging him to subvert the traditional rock star image with an androgynous look that made the critics take notice.

They married a year after they met and Duncan Zowie Haywood Jones was born in May 1971. Recalling the time before their son's birth in her autobiography, Angie described Bowie as a model parent: "David was so sweet, the typical devoted hippie husband and father-to-be, all concern and involvement. When he wasn't out on the road or adventuring in America he even came with me to the clinic for my checkups."

Bowie celebrated the birth of his son on his next album, *Hunky Dory*, with the song "Kooks."

Keeping up with the Joneses—
David and Angie, not your typical
suburban newlyweds. Bowie wrote in
"Kooks," "Don't pick fights with the
bullies and the cads. Because I'm not
much cop at punching other people's
dads." And you've got to believe him.

I bought you a pair of shoes
A trumpet you can blow
And a book of rules
On what to say to people when they
    pick on you
'Cause if you stay with us you're gonna
    be pretty Kookie too

The young Duncan/Zowie Jones with Dad, a couple of image changes later. The red hair lasted a lot longer than the eye patch.

Angie had wanted to call their son Zoe (Greek for "life") but settled for the less feminine Zowie. Bowie had started life as David Jones, but after the success of British singer Davy Jones in the Monkees, opted for Bowie (pronounced "bo-ee", not "bow-ee").

But the young Duncan Jones's life was unsettled almost from birth. The experience had left Angie with a cracked pelvis and 38 stitches and when her friend Dana Gillespie declared she looked as white as a sheet and needed sunshine, she decided to go off to Lake Maggiore for six days. She hired a nanny and went. "David, I think, was appalled by what

Angie Bowie didn't hang around to play the kookie parent role for long. David eventually got custody of his son.

I'd done, horrified that I could get up and leave my baby boy the way I had."

In the years that followed, Angie and David explored their style and their sexuality with Bowie's career reaching stratospheric proportions. Duncan, who used the name Zowie, then Joey, and then Joe, had no option but "to take a chance with a couple of Kooks"—but it was usually just one kook, Bowie, or his Scottish nanny. Angie was the partying type, not the mothering type.

Looking back, Bowie admits he could have done better as a father: "My son's seen me through some of the most awful depressing times when I was really in absolute abject agony over my emotional state; the heights of my drinking and drug-taking. He's seen the lot." Angie and David divorced in 1980, when Duncan was nine, and it was the singer who got custody.

Surprisingly, for the sensitive Bowie, he sent his son to the tough, no-frills boarding school Gordonstoun in Scotland, where Prince Charles had been educated. "It was a bit like that Monty Python sketch where they make you go out and lick the road," said Duncan years afterwards. There would certainly be none of the casual attitude to school as envisioned in the song.

> And if the homework brings you down,
> Then we'll throw it on the fire and take the car downtown

At 18, Zowie, Joey, Joe became Duncan once more and set off on what would be a long road to find a career. He spent years as a student both in England and Ohio where he gained a degree in Philosophy from Wooster College. But it was when his father suggested he come along to the set of a film he was starring in with Catherine Deneuve—*The Hunger*, directed by Tony (*Top Gun*) Scott—that he found something he really wanted to do. He was given the brief to rove the set with a "wild camera." He applied to the London Film School and after graduating began to take film jobs. In 2009 his first feature film, *Moon*, won him a BAFTA (the British equivalent of an Oscar) as Best Newcomer. He went on to direct the 2011 Jake Gyllenhaal film *Source Code*.

When Angie saw his initial success, *Moon*, she commented: "I felt only one overriding emotion and that was grief. My son is messed up. The film is about one man's isolation and confusion and I now realise, through Zowie's art, what a mistake I made leaving him."

Duncan's reaction? "I think she also said it was about her, which figures."

DAVID BOWIE's career has been typified by innovation and experimentation. He has received unparalleled critical and commercial acclaim from the late 1960s onward. "Kooks" featured on his 1971 album *Hunky Dory*.

Bowie would go on to have seven UK chart-topping albums over two decades, illustrating his longevity. His numerous reinventions, including the "Berlin Trilogy" of albums that so inspired the 1980s synthesizer bands, kept his career alive for 40 years. He declined a knighthood in 2002, stating "I would never have any intention of accepting anything like that. I seriously don't know what it's for. It's not what I spent my life working for." A heart attack in 2004, after which he underwent emergency angioplasty to unblock an artery, saw him effectively retire from recording and performing, but indebted newcomers like Lady Gaga will ensure he is not forgotten.

The Last Time
I Saw Richard

Joni Mitchell

With the release in 1971 of her album *Blue*, Joni Mitchell demonstrated a new maturity in her songwriting. It followed a year away from the demands of touring and recording; Mitchell withdrew to concentrate on painting and travel. The decision gave her the space to reflect and develop, and the result was an album widely regarded as one of the best collections of introspective, confessional songs ever released.

Many of the songs explore emotionally intense episodes of her life, seeking to understand and draw a line under them. "My Old Man" (see page 90) was written after the painful end of her affair with Graham Nash. "Little Green" is an achingly honest reflection on the daughter she gave up for adoption in 1965. The album's closing track, "The Last Time I Saw Richard," looks back to the failure of her first marriage.

In 1964 Joni, then Joan Anderson, found herself pregnant by Brad MacMath, an ex-boyfriend from art college in Alberta. By then she had migrated to Toronto, Ontario to sing folk music, and there she met another traditional singer, Chuck Mitchell. Chuck is the Richard in the song. The pair struck up a friendship, and when Joni's daughter Kelly was born in February 1965, Chuck took mother and child into his apartment.

Chuck and Joni Mitchell. It was a short-lived duo, but she kept the surname.

Joni could not support a child on her own and was reluctant to tell her parents -about an illegitimate pregnancy. Instead, she and Chuck embarked on a marriage of convenience a few weeks after the birth. They began performing as a duo, Chuck and Joni Mitchell, but when daughter and musical career proved incompatible, Kelly was given up for adoption.

The couple moved to Detroit in the summer of 1965 in pursuit of gigs. But the marriage, based on a child who was no longer in their lives, gradually fell apart. Moreover, the two had very different approaches to folk music.

Musical differences and a daughter that no longer bound them spelled the end of the relationship.

Joni's confessional, emotional style was at odds with Chuck's more intellectual repertoire—he sang traditional ballads and Brecht songs. "I was anti-intellectual to the max," admits Joni. "Chuck always said that you couldn't write unless you read. He considered me an illiterate, and he didn't give me a great deal of encouragement."

In 1967 the professional and personal partnership was dissolved, although they met sporadically around town over the next year or so before Joni moved to New York. In the song, Joni remembers Chuck's taunt about her romanticism when she finds herself brooding temporarily in a dimly lit coffeehouse booth, but it's

> Only a dark cocoon before I get my gorgeous wings and fly away
> Only a phase, these dark café days

Joni kept Chuck's surname but ignored his opinion and wrote the songs that made her the voice of her generation.

Their daughter Kelly became curious about the identity of her mother in the 1990s, and she and Joni were eventually reunited in 1997. Chuck Mitchell still performs—his set still includes traditional Irish and Scottish folksongs alongside the works of Flanders and Swann and Brecht and Weill.

JONI MITCHELL more or less completed her connection with the confessional singer-songwriter genre with the *Blue* album. "There's hardly a dishonest note in the vocals," she said in 1979, adding: "At that period of my life, I had no personal defenses. ... I felt like I had absolutely no secrets from the world and I couldn't pretend in my life to be strong. Or to be happy." "The Last Time I Saw Richard" was sometimes played in concert as a medley with Dylan's "Mr. Tambourine Man," and a recording exists of a duet with her boyfriend of the time, James Taylor.

Let Me Roll It
Paul McCartney & Wings

In 1971 the breakdown in the relationship between John Lennon and Paul McCartney was complete. Perhaps it's true that the group that plays together, stays together. The Beatles had stopped touring in 1966, and without the teamwork required of live performances, artistic tensions began to arise. These tensions were further exploited by the death of their influential manager Brian Epstein in 1967. The Beatles could not agree on a replacement and their business affairs, including Apple Corps, descended into chaos.

Pink Floyd settled their differences, but the rift between Lennon and McCartney never healed.

On top of all that, the partners of Lennon and McCartney, Yoko Ono and Linda Eastman, were felt to be exerting an increasing and unwelcome influence on the band's creative output. An atmosphere of animosity prevailed. When Paul McCartney announced in April 1970 at the launch of his first solo album that he was leaving the Beatles, he effectively killed off the band.

As a result, Lennon held McCartney entirely responsible for the end of the group. "No one wants to be the one to say the party's over," he later commented. He wrote a bitter attack against his old friend with the song "How Do You Sleep?" (see page 40). A long, sad period of estrangement followed between the two men jointly responsible for some of the world's greatest pop songs. McCartney made repeated efforts to reconnect, all rejected by Lennon.

"Let Me Roll It," from the 1973 album *Band on the Run*, is seen by fans as one of several songs written by McCartney as a riposte to Lennon's musical assault on him. The echo-heavy vocal style of the track is interpreted as a parody of Lennon's use of rock'n'roll reverb in recordings. The lyrics are, however, more conciliatory than aggressive, perhaps describing Paul's attempts to get through to John.

Paul has never confirmed or denied that the song was about John, and in 1993 he claimed not to have noticed that the vocal production sounded like Lennon's. Others have simplistically seen the song as a (not very) veiled reference to drugs. Some suggest that it's "No Words" from the same album that replies to Lennon:

> You want to turn your head away ...
> I wish you'd see, it's only me, I love you

"It's only me" was a phrase cherished by Paul since John had once used it to cool things down during an argument.

Although there was to be no great reconciliation between John and Paul, by the end of the 1970s the pair were on guardedly friendly speaking terms again, at least by telephone. The story goes that on April 25, 1976, Lennon had to ask Paul to stop turning up at his New York apartment in the Dakota building with a guitar in the hope of reconnecting musically. "Please call before you come over," Lennon told McCartney. It was the last time they met. John Lennon was shot and killed on the steps of the Dakota on December 8, 1980.

PAUL McCARTNEY was the man who split up the Beatles at the beginning of the 1970s, embarking on a solo career that hit many highs and lows.

Band on the Run, **on which "Let Me Roll It" appears, was the last McCartney album issued on the Apple label. It was 1974's top-selling studio album in the United Kingdom and United States, and revitalized McCartney's critical standing, a contemporary review in** *Rolling Stone* **magazine describing it as "the finest record yet released by any of the four musicians who were once called the Beatles."**

Life in a Northern Town
Dream Academy

It is not clear whether Nick Drake took his own life or died following an accidental overdose of antidepressants in 1974. Out of contract with his record company, yet anxious to record a fourth album, the singer had just split up with his girlfriend and was back living at home with his parents. His death was not a major event in the music business. His first three albums had sold little more than 5,000 copies each. Yet in the intervening years since his death they have come to be regarded as some of the most influential folk-rock albums of the 1970s. Such is his enduring appeal that in 2010 original producer Joe Boyd put together a tribute to his music, *Way to Blue*. It was an evening of Nick Drake songs featuring a full orchestra and a variety of guest vocalists, including Robyn Hitchcock, Green Gartside of Scritti Politti, Lisan Hannigan, Krystle Warren, and Teddy Thompson. Ironically, it played to more people in a few days than Drake had performed to in his lifetime.

Drake as he appeared on the cover of his debut album Five Leaves Left.

Nick Laird-Clowes recalled the night in 1984 when he and Dream Academy comember Gilbert Gabriel composed "Life in a Northern Town." "Two guitars—one nylon strung with just three strings on it, while the other was the same guitar that was on the cover of Nick Drake's *Bryter Layter*. We had the idea, even before we sat down, to write a folk song with an African-style chorus. We started it and when we got to the verse melody, there was something about it that reminded me of Nick Drake. I was working at the RCA record factory in Ladbroke Grove at the time and bought Nick Drake's guitar for £100. When the single was completed I dedicated it to Nick." The song went on to become a Top 10 hit in the US, spawning renewed interest in Nick Drake's musical legacy.

Drake had left Cambridge University before finishing his degree in English Literature and signed a three-album deal with Island Records. His first album, *Five Leaves Left*, had a favorable reception in the music press but suffered from Drake's chronic shyness and inability to play live and promote it.

On his second album, *Bryter Layter*, producer Joe Boyd enlisted the help of the Velvet Underground's John Cale to play piano and organ on one of the stand-out tracks, "Northern Sky," which would be the inspiration for the Dream Academy song. Even though Island Records thought the album would have commercial success, Drake, now smoking what his college friend and music arranger Robert Kirby described as "unbelievable amounts" of marijuana, refused to do press interviews, radio sessions, or live appearances.

Pink Moon, the follow-up to *Bryter Layter*, was recorded in two nights with just Drake playing guitar. He delivered it to the record company out of the blue. It sold less than the previous albums and Island declined the idea of a fourth.

Drake descended into a lonely, uncommunicative period of drifting, with spells in the hospital to cope with his depression. Although his death was not officially confirmed as suicide, his sister, actress Gabrielle Drake, prefers to think that it was: "I'd rather he died because he wanted to end it than it to be the result of a tragic mistake. That would seem to me to be terrible."

DREAM ACADEMY failed to repeat the success of their David Gilmour–produced first single. Follow-up "The Love Parade" failed to chart in the UK and the group officially split in 1991. Nick Laird-Clowes worked again with Gilmour on the lyrics for Pink Floyd's *The Division Bell* before recording a solo album. Gilbert Gabriel and Kate St. John have since recorded together as the Believers.

Love Kills
The Ramones

In July 1976, Sid Vicious saw the Ramones live for the first time. A then-unknown member of the Sex Pistols entourage, Vicious showed his appreciation by hurling a bottle at singer Joey Ramone during the gig at London's Dingwalls. Eighteen months later, New Year's Eve 1977, he was happily hanging out backstage at their gig at the Rainbow Theatre in Finsbury Park.

A full-fledged Sex Pistol, Sid was now more famous than his heroes, but he loyally said, "The Ramones are my favorite group."

Vicious was particularly enamored with Ramones bassist Dee Dee. Manager Danny Fields recalled that "Sid idolized Dee Dee. He was his role model, a junkie bass player who was marginally more competent than Sid." Like Dee Dee, Sid played his bass low-slung and, according to Fields, both men shared the belief that "to be a perfect rock star, you have to be a complete wreck."

John Simon Ritchie, a college buddy of Johnny Rotten, had been nicknamed Sid Vicious after the Pistols' singer's pet hamster. Sid's embodiment of the punk ethos allowed him to replace sacked bassist Glen Matlock early in 1977; his inability to play bass was not regarded as a problem. He did make some attempt to master the instrument, initially by repeatedly playing along to the Ramones' first album.

In March 1977, Sid met Nancy Spungen, an American groupie who had moved to London in search of a punk beau. Together, Sid and Nancy descended into the netherworld of addiction. After the Sex Pistols disintegrated on tour in America

Sid Vicious trailed by girlfriend Nancy Spungen, whom he would later kill.

in 1978, Sid made sporadic, abortive attempts to start a solo career. He spoke of forming a band with Dee Dee, although the Ramones bassist was unaware of Sid's intention.

On October 12, 1978, Nancy Spungen was found dead in a pool of blood in the couple's room in Manhattan's notorious Chelsea Hotel. Vicious was arrested and charged with her murder. He claimed to have no recollection of the incident, and mystery surrounds what happened.

Dee Dee stood by his friend, buying Sid a new padlock and chain which he wore around his neck like a pendant, as the New York Police Department had confiscated the original. Released on bail and awaiting trial, Vicious fatally overdosed on heroin on February 2, 1979.

Sid's death moved Dee Dee to pen "Love Kills," a tribute to Vicious and his equally notorious girlfriend Nancy Spungen. Dee Dee unusually takes the lead vocal on the song, a characteristically short and high-octane Ramones number. "Love Kills" adopts the theory that it was a bungled suicide pact.

The notion of the doomed couple as a punk rock Romeo and Juliet also informed director Alex Cox's biopic *Sid and Nancy*, sometimes subtitled *Love Kills*.

THE RAMONES' 1976 debut album and visit to London that year proved a seminal influence on a generation of English punk bands. 1977's *Leave Home* gave them a UK hit single in "Sheena Is a Punk Rocker." Their ninth album, *Animal Boy*, was released in 1986 and featured "Love Kills." The band split up in 1995 after 14 studio albums. Dee Dee Ramone took a fatal heroin overdose in 2002, shortly after the band was inducted into the Rock and Roll Hall of Fame. His death came a year after that of singer Joey Ramone. Two years later, founding member Johnny Ramone died.

The Ramones' modest commercial success is inversely proportionate to their influence on punk, indie, and hardcore.

Luka
Suzanne Vega

Suzanne Vega chose music over her first love, dance, and it's the rhythm of words that has driven her ever since. She also admits to devouring textbooks on science and medical matters for inspiration.

When Vega was two and a half, the family moved from her birthplace in California to New York City. She grew up in Spanish Harlem and the Upper West Side.

Following chart success in the UK, 1987's "Luka" (a US Billboard #3) broke her into her home country at last, helping Suzanne's second LP garner three Grammy nominations.

Horatio Street in Greenwich Village, where Vega was living when she first spotted Luka.

Her ability to write in character made "Luka,"a song sung by an abused child, so gripping. She admits Lou Reed's similarly themed 1973 album *Berlin* was an influence, and that she had been listening to it on the day she wrote, "probably to sharpen and focus myself." Having spent "a good few months" thinking about it, she wrote the song in just two hours.

The story is partly based on a real child who lived in her New York neighborhood and who she used to see as one of a group of children playing in front of her building. "Luka seemed a little bit distinctive from the other children. I always remembered his name, and I always remembered his face, and I didn't know much about him, but he just seemed set apart from these other children that I would see playing. And his character is what I based the song on. In the song, the boy Luka is an abused child, in real life I don't think he was. I think he was just different."

In an interview with *The Performing Songwriter* magazine she likened the compositional process to writing a play. "First of all, how do you introduce the character? You do that by saying, my name is Luka, I live on the second floor. And then you get the audience involved, saying, I live upstairs from you. So you've seen me before. You're incriminating the audience. You're pointing the finger without really doing it. You're unfolding this story that can't really be told and you're involving the audience in it and that was what I wanted to do."

In 1996, a decade after writing the song, she revealed that, by coincidence, Luka shared her surname, Vega, and that, far from stigmatizing him, the song had made him a local celebrity. "After the song became popular, I heard from my old roommate who said that he had come back to my old apartment with a girl … he must have been 15 or 16. He asked my roommate, 'Would you please, tell this girl that Suzanne Vega really *did* live here.' He didn't seem traumatized by it. He was using it to get girlfriends as far as I could see."

When *Musician* magazine featured Vega in 1988, they included her as a member of a so-called wave of women performers making their mark: Sinead O'Connor, Tracy Chapman, Michelle Shocked, and Toni Childs were her contemporaries. Her consistent release of new material has outlasted the competition.

SUZANNE VEGA was born in 1959 and graduated from the legendary New York High School for the Performing Arts (on which the movie *Fame* was based) in 1977. She chose the city's Greenwich Village folk-club circuit as her finishing school. Within two years of signing her record contract in 1984, she was playing a pair of sold-out dates at London's Royal Albert Hall.

Her biggest hit, "Tom's Diner," was originally the acappella lead track from her album *Solitude Standing*. It was reworked by British dance act DNA in 1990 and gave her an unexpected but welcome transatlantic Top 5 hit. It's since undergone 30 remixes.

Magic Man
Heart

Despite repeated denials, Heart are still plagued by rumors that their 1976 hit "Magic Man" was written for murderous cult leader Charles Manson, or that the profits from its sales were sent to Manson in prison, or that messages of support for Manson were encoded on the covers of early Heart releases. None of these stories is true. The song actually harks back to a heady romance in the early days of the group's formation.

Heart's lead vocalist, Ann Wilson, started out, along with Roger Fisher (the group's original guitarist) and Steve Fossen (its first bass player) in an earlier group called Hocus Pocus, playing clubs in the northwestern United States. Roger's brother Mike had, like many young American men, dodged the Vietnam draft by fleeing over the border to Canada. One weekend in late 1971 Mike traveled secretly back to the US to see his brother's band perform and met Ann for the first time. They immediately fell in love. It was a powerful moment. Ann dropped everything and followed Mike

Nice hair. The Heart line-up in 1976—the year that saw them score their first US Top Ten hit with "Magic Man."

Fisher back across the border; "Magic Man" describes their first year together. It contrasts the plea from Ann's mother for her daughter to "Come on home, girl" back to Seattle, with Mike's invitation to Ann to "Come on home, girl" to Vancouver as his lover.

The following year, first Fossen and then Mike's brother Roger followed them into Canada, and in 1973 they formed Heart. At first the line-up featured both Fisher brothers on guitars, but in 1974 Ann's sister Nancy also moved to Canada and joined the band. The presence of the two Wilson girls became the band's distinctive feature and its main selling point. Their multi-instrumental abilities also allowed Mike to withdraw from performance duties and adopt a backstage role as the band's sound and lighting engineer, and later as their manager.

"Magic Man" remains, according to Ann Wilson, Heart's most requested song. It owes its success in part to Roger Fisher's mystical rock guitar lines; but mostly to Ann's lyrical expression of a classic rite of passage. From childhood to adulthood, from living with your parents to living with your lover, what teenager in love hasn't yelled at some point, "Try to understand!"

Ann, who later raised two adopted children as a single mother, has had no "significant other" since she and her Magic Man split in 1979.

HEART were blighted by record-company hassles that prevented their capitalizing on the 1976 success of "Magic Man"—a US Billboard #9 single. They took a decade to find the formula for sustained success but were rewarded for their perseverance as, with a second change of record label to Capitol, they perfected the AOR power ballad. Two fine examples of this, "These Dreams" and "Alone," topped the US chart in 1986 and 1987, and significantly, both were from outside writing teams. Meanwhile "Magic Man," always a live highlight, lived on; it was sampled by rapper Ice-T, featured in several computer games, and featured on the soundtrack of Sofia Coppola's 1999 film *The Virgin Suicides.*

Malibu
Hole

Courtney Love met Kurt Cobain on January 12, 1990, in Portland's Satyricon nightclub when they both still led aspiring underground rock bands. Love fronted her own band Hole while Cobain was the driving force behind Seattle's grunge favorites Nirvana. Love made advances, but Cobain was evasive. Early in their liaison, Cobain broke off dates and ignored Love's phone calls because he was unsure he wanted a relationship. Cobain noted, "I was determined to be a bachelor for a few months. … But I knew that I liked Courtney so much right away that it was a really hard struggle to stay away from her for so many months."

Around the time of Nirvana's 1992 performance on *Saturday Night Live*, Love discovered that she was pregnant with Cobain's child. On February 24, 1992, a few days after the conclusion of Nirvana's Pacific Rim tour, they were married on Waikiki Beach in Hawaii. Love wore a satin and lace dress once owned by the actress Frances Farmer, and Cobain wore green pajamas, because he had been "too lazy to put on a tux." In an interview with *The Guardian*, Love revealed the opposition to their marriage from various people: "Kim Gordon of Sonic Youth sits me down and says, 'If you marry him your life is not going to happen, it will destroy your life.' But I said, 'Whatever! I love him, and I want to be with him!'"

On August 18, 1992, the couple's daughter Frances Bean Cobain was born. In a *Vanity Fair* article, Love had admitted using heroin while unknowingly pregnant. Cobain and Love's romance had always been a media attraction; now they found themselves hounded by tabloid reporters after the article was published, many wanting to know if Frances was addicted to drugs at birth. The Los Angeles County Department of Children's Services took the Cobains to court, claiming that the couple's drug usage made them unfit parents. Two-week-old Frances was ordered by the judge to be taken from their custody and placed with Courtney's sister Jamie for several weeks, after which the couple obtained custody in an exchange agreement to submit to urine tests and regular visits from a social worker. After months of legal wrangling, the couple were eventually granted full custody of their daughter.

Throughout most of his life, Cobain suffered from chronic bronchitis and intense physical pain due to an undiagnosed chronic stomach condition. Cobain's cousin Beverly, a nurse, claimed Cobain was diagnosed with attention-deficit-hyperactivity disorder as a child, and bipolar disorder as an adult. She also brought attention to the history of suicide, mental

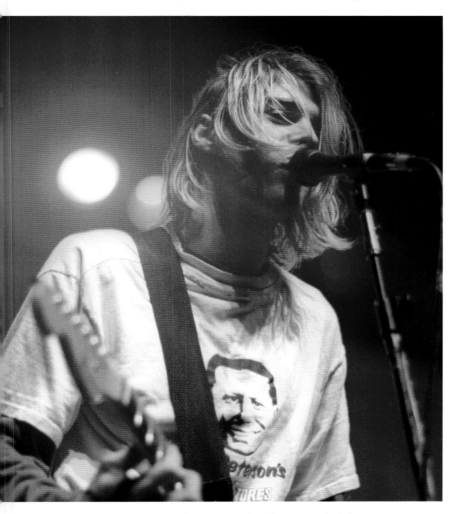

Cobain performing onstage with Nirvana at the Salem Armory in Salem, December 14, 1993.

illness, and alcoholism in the Cobain family, noting two of her uncles who had committed suicide with guns.

Cobain's first experience with heroin occurred some time in 1986, administered to him by a local drug dealer in Tacoma, Washington, who had previously supplied him with Percodan. He used heroin sporadically for several years, but, by the end of 1990, his use developed into a full-fledged addiction. Cobain claimed that he was "determined to get a habit" as a way to self-medicate his stomach condition. "It started with three days in a row of doing heroin and I don't have a stomach pain. That was such a relief," he related.

Cobain's heroin addiction worsened. His first attempt at rehab was made in early 1992, not long after he and Love discovered they were going to become parents. Immediately after leaving rehab, Nirvana embarked on their Australian tour with Cobain appearing pale and gaunt while suffering through withdrawals. Not long after returning home, Cobain's heroin use resumed.

Prior to a performance at the New Music Seminar in New York City in July 1993, Cobain suffered a heroin overdose. Rather than calling for an ambulance, Love injected Cobain with Narcan to bring him out of his unconscious state. Cobain proceeded to perform with Nirvana,

HOLE formed in L.A. in 1989 with Eric Erlandson (guitar), Jill Emery (bass), Caroline Rue (drums), and Courtney Love (lead singer and songwriter). Love's lyrical concerns ranged from sleaze to sex but "Malibu," from 1998's *Celebrity Skin* album, was more personal. *Celebrity Skin*, the band's third studio album, moved away from Hole's harder alternative rock past toward a cleaner, more radio-friendly pop rock format. It was not only their most commercially successful album but also the last album before their split in 2002.

Love, who has remained in the public eye for increasingly non-musical reasons, reformed the band in 2010.

giving the public no indication that anything out of the ordinary had taken place.

Following a tour stop in Munich, Germany, on March 1, 1994, Cobain was diagnosed with bronchitis and severe laryngitis. He flew to Rome the next day for medical treatment, and was joined there by his wife on March 3, 1994. The next morning, Love awoke to find that Cobain had overdosed on a combination of champagne and Rohypnol. Cobain was immediately rushed to the hospital and spent the rest of the day unconscious. After five days in the hospital, Cobain was released and returned to Seattle. Love later stated that the incident was Cobain's first suicide attempt.

Courtney Love, holding daughter Frances Bean Cobain, along with Kurt at the MTV-Video Music Awards in September 1993.

On March 18, 1994, Love phoned Seattle police informing them that Cobain was suicidal and had locked himself in a room with a gun. Police arrived and confiscated several guns and a bottle of pills from Cobain, who insisted that he was not suicidal and had locked himself in the room to hide from Love. When questioned by police, Love said that Cobain had never mentioned that he was suicidal and that she had not seen him with a gun.

Love arranged an intervention regarding Cobain's drug use on March 25, 1994. The ten people involved included musician friends, record company executives, and one of Cobain's closest friends, Dylan Carlson. The intervention was initially unsuccessful, with an angry Cobain insulting and heaping scorn on its participants and eventually locking himself in the upstairs bedroom. However, by the end of the day, Cobain had agreed to undergo a detox program. Cobain arrived at the Exodus Recovery Center in Marina del Rey, California, on March 30, 1994. The staff at the facility were unaware of Cobain's history of depression and prior attempts at suicide. When visited by friends, there was no indication to them that Cobain was in any negative or suicidal state of mind. He spent the day talking to counselors about his drug abuse and personal problems, and happily playing with his daughter Frances. These interactions were the last time she would see her father. The following night, Cobain walked outside to have a cigarette and climbed over a six-foot-high fence to leave the facility. He took a taxi to Los Angeles Airport and flew back to Seattle. On the flight he sat next to Duff McKagan of Guns N' Roses. Despite Cobain's own personal animosity towards Guns N' Roses, and specifically Axl Rose, Cobain "seemed happy" to see McKagan. On April 3, 1994, Love contacted a private investigator, Tom Grant, and hired him to find Cobain. On April 7, 1994, amid rumors of Nirvana breaking up, the band pulled out of that year's Lollapalooza music festival.

On April 8, 1994, at the age of 27, Cobain's body was discovered at his Lake Washington home by an electrician who had arrived to install a security system. Apart from a minor amount of blood coming out of Cobain's ear, the electrician reported seeing no visible signs of trauma, and initially believed that Cobain was asleep until he saw the shotgun pointing at his chin. A suicide note was found, addressed to Cobain's childhood imaginary friend "Boddah," that said, paraphrasing, "I haven't felt the excitement of listening to as well as creating music, along with really writing ... for too many years now." A high concentration of heroin and traces of Valium were also found in his body. Cobain's body had been lying there for days; the coroner's report estimated Cobain to have died on April 5, 1994.

Courtney Love's song "Malibu" was recorded after Cobain's death and included on the *Celebrity Skin* album released in 1998. It includes poignant references to the singer's battle with his demons and the relief he sought in heroin. "How are you so burnt when you're barely on fire." Love told *Blender* magazine, "When I was pregnant, Kurt and I always had this thing about getting out of the basement apartment we lived in, with dealers next door, and going to live in Malibu. It's a very healing place." The song was nominated for a Grammy in 1999 and reached #3 on the Billboard Alternative chart.

It is a far more fitting Hole tribute than their 1994 song "Rock Star" with the lyric: "So much fun to be Nirvana/Barrel of laughs to be Nirvana/ Say you'd rather die."

Cobain's artistic endeavors and struggles with heroin addiction, illness, and depression, as well as the circumstances of his death, have become a frequent topic of fascination, debate, and controversy throughout the music world. In death, Cobain became one of the 27 Club, along with Brian Jones, Jimi Hendrix, Jim Morrison, Janis Joplin, and latterly Amy Winehouse—rock stars who checked out at 27.

When the electrician called at Cobain's waterside home to install a security system, he thought at first that the singer was asleep.

Man on the Moon
R.E.M.

As the 1980s turned into the 1990s, R.E.M., standard-bearers of jangling guitar rock, seemed unstoppable. "Man on the Moon" was the second single to be taken from their 1992 platinum-selling *Automatic for the People* LP. The album had started out the year before at rehearsals held without singer Michael Stipe, where the band swapped instruments—Peter Buck on mandolin instead of guitar, Mills playing piano instead of bass, and Bill Berry swapping drums for bass.

When the trio presented demos of some 30 new songs to Stipe, the singer told *Rolling Stone* that they were "very mid-tempo … pretty fucking weird." The album deals with loss and mortality, a theme fueled by the constantly circulating (and happily false) rumor that Stipe might be dying of an AIDS-related illness.

Written by all four founding members of the band, "Man on the Moon" was a reference to the conspiracy theory that the six manned missions to the Moon (1969–72) were hoaxes staged by NASA. Conspiracy-mongers claim that the film of the missions was made using similar sets to those used in the astronaut training simulations on Earth, like the Mars landing in the 1970s film *Capricorn One*. The space race was a part of the Cold War era and America had to get to the moon ahead of the Soviets. They believed the landings had to be faked to realize John F. Kennedy's 1961 vision of "fulfilling the goal, before this decade is out, of landing a man on the moon and returning him safely to Earth." Such an achievement would have been vital as a distraction to Americans disillusioned with the escalating war in Vietnam at the end of the 1960s.

The song was inspired by Andy Kaufman, a "Dadaistic" comedian and actor who took performance art and comedy to the edge of irrationality and blurred the borders between imagination and reality. As a teenager, Michael Stipe saw him on TV and cites him as a huge influence.

Kaufman, born in New York in 1949, honed his style of stand-up comedy in the nightclubs and coffeehouses of his hometown before being asked by Lorne Michaels to appear in the first broadcast of what was to become the immensely popular and successful TV show *Saturday Night Live,* first broadcast on October 11, 1975.

Kaufman was a huge fan of Elvis Presley, and by the time the funnyman was in high school he'd got his impersonations of the King down pat. Many say that he was the first Elvis impersonator—Andy even hitchhiked to Las Vegas to see his idol—and the King considered the impersonation of him his favorite. Stipe makes reference to this in the second line of the second verse:

> Hey Andy, are you goofing on Elvis?
> Hey baby, are we losing touch?

Also referred to in the song was Kaufman's love of pro wrestling— Andy was the world's first intergender wrestling champion, wrestling over 400 women between 1979 and 1983. The line "Mr. Blassie in a breakfast mess" refers to a film Kaufman made in 1983, *My Breakfast with Blassie,* directed by Linda Lautrec and Johnny Legend. This hour-long faux doc, a spoof on Louis Malle's *My Breakfast with Andre*, sees the comic meet up with retired heavyweight wrestler "Classy" Freddie Blassie for 60 minutes of excruciatingly awkward conversation. The film was ultimately most notable for Kaufman meeting his girlfriend Lynn Marguiles on set.

Andy Kaufman's role in Taxi *as hapless cabbie Latkas Gravas was written for him after producers saw his "Foreign Man" comedy character.*

Kaufman debuts "Foreign Man" on **Van Dyke and Company** *in 1976. The comedian was fond of elaborate practical jokes—many thought he had faked his own premature death.*

After being catapulted to fame via *Saturday Night Live*, Kaufman landed a plum role as Latka Gravas in the TV sitcom *Taxi*. Sadly, at the height of his fame, the comic died on the evening of May 16, 1984, of a rare form of lung cancer—though rumors initially circulated that he had staged his own death.

The "Man on the Moon" video by Peter Care was shot in California's Antelope Valley and depicts Michael Stipe wearing a cowboy hat and walking along a desert road. He's picked up by a man in a truck (Bill Berry) and taken to a truckstop where Peter Buck is the barman and Mike Mills is playing pool. After eating a plate of fries, Stipe walks off into the night. In the background of the truckstop is a TV set showing various clips of Andy Kaufman.

British 1970s glam rockers Mott the Hoople are mentioned in the opening line, but in 2004, in response to a question on his website, former Mott lead singer Ian Hunter could shed no light on their inclusion. Hunter laconically quipped, "Beats me!"

The lyrics explore perceptions of reality and illusion and how beliefs become reality. They cite examples such as Newton's theory of gravity and Darwin's challenging of religious beliefs with his theory of evolution.

The song is made more appealing by the extensive use of the "yeah, yeah, yeahs" at the end of each line of the verses. On an edition of the British chart show *Top of the Pops 2*, Stipe was quoted as saying that they were included as a tribute to the music and writing of Kurt Cobain. It was the singer's attempt to outdo the Nirvana frontman's own predilection for trying to squeeze as many "yeahs" into a song as possible—Cobain was a master at trying to get them to fit.

The song lent its title to a 1999 film about Kaufman, directed by Milos Forman and starring Jim Carrey, Danny De Vito, and Courtney Love, for which R.E.M. created the soundtrack. Michael Stipe has said that he sees the song as a "funny, sad eulogy to a very great man." R.E.M. performed the song with Pearl Jam's Eddie Vedder when they were inducted into the Rock and Roll Hall of Fame in 2007.

R.E.M., a Georgia four-piece named after the optical Rapid Eye Movement phenomenon, made the transition from college radio favorites to global superstars in a decade. Two contrasting hit singles, "Losing My Religion" and "Shiny Happy People" had broken through before their eighth album, 1992's *Automatic for the People*, which yielded a staggering six more, including "Man on the Moon." In 1997 the quartet reinvented the R.E.M. sound by incorporating drum machines and synthesizers, but the departure of drummer Bill Berry was a body blow. In September 2011 the band announced they were "calling it a day."

The Man with the Child in His Eyes

Kate Bush

Television and radio presenter Steve Blacknell is perhaps best known for interviewing Phil Collins on the Concorde between the singing drummer's transatlantic Live Aid appearances in 1985. In spite of a substantial career in the media spotlight, it was not until 2010 that Blacknell revealed that he was the inspiration for Kate Bush's song "The Man with the Child in His Eyes."

Bush had begun playing piano at age 10. She immersed herself in music, writing 200 songs by the time she was 16, something she avoided mentioning to boyfriends. "It would always cause trouble. They'd think I was cleverer than them or something daft like that—I was a threat to their masculinity."

She met Blacknell in the mid-1970s when he was a toilet cleaner in a nearby mental hospital in Bexley, Kent. "By the spring of 1975 she had become my first true love," he recalled. Six years older than Kate, he was not threatened by her talent, and he introduced her to the music of the Incredible String Band and rock instrumentalists Camel. They also shared dreams, "She had her heart set on becoming a global star and I was going to be a flash DJ. One day I would introduce her on *Top of the Pops*."

> He's very understanding
> And he's so aware of all my situations

Nevertheless, Bush remained protective of her work and Blacknell resolved to wait until the moment was right to experience it. "In the summer of 1975, I finally got my break and landed a job as a marketing assistant with Decca Records. It was then that I finally thought I was equipped to hear her music and it was a day I'll never forget. I went round to her house and she led me to the room where the piano was. I thought 'Oh my God.' What I heard made my soul stand on end. I realized there and then that I was in love with a genius."

Blacknell finally spoke about their relationship when he decided to sell the handwritten lyrics to "The Man with the Child in His Eyes," a gift from Kate to him. The manuscript was auctioned on a website specializing in rock'n'roll memorabilia. He explained, "For one reason or another I really haven't talked about it through the years. Of course I have the stories, but Kate was, and is a private person and I respect that." He added, "I've been told by those around her that I was indeed 'The Man with the Child in His Eyes' and I know that those words were given to me by someone very special."

Bush has never publicly discussed the identity of the man in her song, but she has commented on its musical genesis. "The inspiration for 'The Man with the Child in His Eyes' was really just a particular thing that happened when I went to the piano. The piano just started speaking to me." As for the song's theme, "It was a theory that I had had for a while that I just observed in most of the men that I know – the fact that they just are little boys inside and how wonderful it is that they manage to retain this magic."

She later explained, "It's really nice to keep that delight in wonderful things that children have. And that's what I was trying to say. That this man could communicate with a younger girl because he's on the same level."

A photo before Steve Blacknell's media career and Kate Bush's multiplatinum albums. Bush has been successful at keeping most of her private life from the public gaze.

The lyrics also delved into the nature of the attraction between older men and younger women. "I, myself, am attracted to older men, I guess, but I think that's the same with every female. I think it's a very natural, basic instinct that you look continually for your father for the rest of your life, as do men continually look for their mother in the women that they meet. I don't think we're all aware of it, but I think it is basically true. You look for that security that the opposite sex in your parenthood gave you as a child."

Kate was discovered by EMI Records, via Pink Floyd guitarist David Gilmour, when she was 16. The company set up a unique "apprenticeship" scheme for her, nurturing her talent until she was ready for the big time. At 19, she was, as Blacknell had predicted, on *Top of the Pops*. He explained how her success effectively ended their liaison. "As things hotted up for her, so our relationship cooled and we drifted apart."

KATE BUSH's dazzling 1978 debut single "Wuthering Heights," primarily inspired by the movie rather than Emily Bronte's novel, marked the arrival of a unique talent. It was the first self-penned UK #1 by a female artist when Kate was still only 19. Like "The Man with the Child in His Eyes," it was taken from the platinum-selling *The Kick Inside*. Her second album, *Lionheart*, followed nine months later. *Never for Ever* saw her become the first female artist to top the UK album chart. *The Dreaming* (1982) performed less well commercially and critically, but Bush bounced back with the acclaimed *Hounds of Love* in 1985. Gaps between albums grew longer —her next release, *The Red Shoes*, was in 1989.

She took a recording break between 1993's *The Sensual World* and her 2005 comeback, *Aerial*, to bring up her son. In 2011 she surprised fans and critics by releasing two LPs: *Director's Cut*, containing reworkings of earlier material, and *50 Words for Snow*.

"The Man with the Child in His Eyes" was one of the first songs she recorded for her debut album and she admitted to being "terrified" at the prospect of working with a full-scale orchestra during the sessions. She won an important battle with her record company by insisting that the song become the follow-up single to "Wuthering Heights" instead of EMI's choice, "Them Heavy People." That song instead became the lead track on the EP *On Stage*, featuring live recordings from Bush's 1979 tour that was to be her only foray into live performance. Nerves and the physical demands of a two-and-a-half-hour show that included multiple costume changes were partly behind her decision not to repeat the experience. Another factor was the death of lighting engineer Bill Duffield, who was the subject of Bush's song, "Blow Away (For Bill)," which appeared

Kate Bush photographed, age 19, in June 1978. Her debut single "Wuthering Heights" had topped the UK singles charts for a month.

on 1980's *Never Forever*. On the night before her only tour's warm-up date in Poole, in March 1979, 21-year-old Duffield fell 17 feet from a rig while making some final checks on the lights.

Steve Blacknell graduated from marketing man to plugger and A&R man, helping launch the careers of a Flock of Seagulls and Frankie Goes to Hollywood. From there he went into television, becoming a regular on BBC's *Breakfast Time* show. Prior to Live Aid, he was a veejay on MTV. In the UK, he hosted the fondly remembered *Pirate Radio Four* on BBC Radio 4. The late 1980s took him to Hollywood as a presenter and occasional actor. He is now a media consultant and trainer specializing in the music business. A former sufferer of bulimia, he works to help raise awareness of the disease among men.

Memphis
PJ Harvey

Jeff Buckley was in Memphis, Tennessee, working on songs for a new album. On the evening of May 29, 1997, while awaiting the arrival

Jeff Buckley's musical legacy was just a single studio album.

of his band, he went swimming, as he had many times before, in Wolf River, a tributary of the Mississippi. Fully clothed and wearing boots, Buckley was singing the chorus of Led Zeppelin's "Whole Lotta Love" as he waded in. He disappeared from view and was caught in the wake of a passing boat. Six days later, his body was discovered floating in the water. The verdict of the autopsy was death by accidental drowning, no alcohol or drugs were found in his system. He was 30. Buckley once said, "I'm a flake. … But sometimes it comes in handy, 'cause flakes are good at letting things happen naturally, even if they're disasters, complete disasters."

His father was singer-songwriter Tim Buckley, whom he barely knew and who died of a heroin overdose at age 28, while his mother, Mary Guibert, was a classically trained pianist and cellist. Buckley's only completed studio album, *Grace*, released in 1994, reflected his passion for diverse musical styles and was an impressive showcase for his guitar playing skills and soaring vocals. Although not a huge commercial success, *Grace* was much acclaimed by critics and other musicians. Buckley's influence grew after his death. His version of Leonard Cohen's "Hallelujah" became a bestseller on iTunes in 2008.

Polly Jean Harvey and Jeff Buckley's paths crossed at the Glastonbury Festival on June 24, 1995, on the famous Pyramid Stage. Harvey was higher up the bill, memorably performing in a vivid pink catsuit. Buckley was impressed on two counts, "she's sexy and she reminds you of [legendary bluesman] Howlin' Wolf." He was known to be a fan of her then-current album *To Bring You My Love*. The admiration was mutual.

Harvey composed "Memphis" as her tribute to Buckley in the form of a passionate letter, adapting two lines "I had to send her away/To bring it back again" from "Morning Theft," a song from the album he was putting together at the time of his death, which was released as *Sketches for My Sweetheart the Drunk* in 1998.

"Memphis" is a simple guitar-led elegy, but like many of Harvey's songs, there is an unsettling edge. Harvey is not sentimental or trying to turn Buckley into a legend. "People want to build musicians into mythical beings," she said, disapprovingly. "I firmly disbelieve that one has to be a tortured soul to write good music." She seems to imagine death by drowning not as traumatic but serene: "But oh what a way to go/So peaceful/He's smiling/I'm with you/I'm singing."

Buckley's tragically early death struck a chord in the musical community. "Memphis" was one of more than 20 songs written about it, including "Teardrop" by Massive Attack whose singer, ex-Cocteau Twin Elizabeth Fraser, had been a close friend.

PJ HARVEY exploded onto the indie rock scene in the early 1990s with two acclaimed singles and her 1992 debut album *Dry* drawing rave reviews for the intensity of her performance. After 1993's *Rid of Me*, she parted company with her other band members and went solo for *To Bring You My Love* in 1995. At the same time, she introduced a new element of theatricality into her performances, dressed as a red-clad vamp. "Memphis" was recorded during the sessions for her 2000 Mercury Prize-winning album *Stories from the City, Stories from the Sea*. She became the first two-time Mercury Prize winner with her 2011 album *Let England Shake*.

Michael
Franz Ferdinand

Frenetic Scottish indie rockers Franz Ferdinand burst onto the scene at the beginning of 2004 with the hit single "Take Me Out." The quartet from Glasgow brought an added energy to the emerging British indie scene at the time and stood out for their nerd-chic and slightly camp appearance. You would expect a band named after the Archduke of Austria whose assassination started World War I to court controversy, and the band certainly turned more than a few conservative heads with their fourth single "Michael," released in August 2004.

Frontman Alex Kapranos purrs the opening lyrics to this fast-paced, provocative number, and it is quickly apparent that the track has overt homoerotic overtones. But Kapranos and his bandmates were all straight men, the former enjoying a relationship with Eleanor Friedberger, one half of US indie brother-sister duo the Fiery Furnaces. She would later be mentioned on a Franz Ferdinand track herself, in "Eleanor Put Your Boots On."

Amid the confusion and intrigue among their fans—and a few homophobic rants from others—Kapranos decided to reveal the true inspiration behind the dance-floor filler he'd penned with guitarist Nick McCarthy, perhaps appropriately to UK-based gay magazine *Boyz*.

"It was one night when me and the band were out with friends from Glasgow, and we went to this warehouse dance-party thing called Disco X. It was

Michael Kasparis was so pleased with the song he appeared as himself in the video.

a very debauched night and these two friends got it together in a very sexy way," he revealed.

One of those friends, the real-life Michael—musician Michael Kasparis, who played guitar for Glasgow band V-Twin—was said to be "chuffed to bits" by his newfound infamy.

> Sticky hair, sticky hips, stubble on my sticky lips
> Michael you're the only one I'd ever want

Helping propel it into the charts was a video, filmed in a dingy Berlin basement, in which the real Michael starred as himself. He said: "We had a 20-hour shoot—from 8 am one day until 4 am—and I was filming continuously. It was good fun. In the last scene, I get my arm ripped off by a guy who wants a part of me. I had to be fitted with a prosthetic arm. The little camp dance I do is just me. It wasn't choreographed. That's how I dance."

"Michael" perhaps predictably provided the major talking point for reviews of Franz Ferdinand's self-titled debut, but the liberal *New Musical Express* saw past the furore and proclaimed: "'Michael' may at first appear to be a frank exploration of homoeroticism, but really Alex is just playing at sexual roles in the same way Morrissey enjoyed 20 years ago."

FRANZ FERDINAND emerged from the scene around Glasgow College of Art in 2002, but only drummer Paul Thomson actually attended. Updating the approach of 1970s art-rock bands like Queen and Roxy Music, Alex Kapranos (vocals), Robert Hardy (bass), Nick McCarthy (guitar), and Thomson were also fans of edgy 1980s bands like the Gang of Four and Fire Engines. Their tactic of overlaying winning melodies on funk rhythms took them to mainstream acclaim with their eponymous debut (on which "Michael" appeared) winning the Mercury Music award in 2004.

My Father's Eyes
Eric Clapton

Eric Clapton never knew his father Edward Walter Fryer, a Canadian serviceman stationed in England who had a brief affair with his mother Pat Clapton in 1944. Eric was raised by his grandparents and believed that Pat, only 17 years older than him, was his sister. The truth came out when he was nine years old. Disturbed by the revelations, Eric took introspective refuge in his guitar, and in the music of the blues.

Eric's father died in 1985 unaware that Clapton was his son. He had been a bar-room piano player and sometimes songwriter, drifting from town to town and from woman to woman—several of whom were mothers to his children. Clapton, like his father, has had a long series of relationships with women. Two years after Fryer's death he himself became father to a son, Conor, the result of another brief affair.

Eric had never experienced a father-son relationship, but as he recalled in his biography, "the closest I ever came to looking into my father's eyes was when I looked into my son's eyes."

ERIC CLAPTON included "My Father's Eyes" on the 1998 album *Pilgrim*, produced by Clapton and Simon Climie, formerly one half of pop duo Climie Fisher. It was released as a single and reached the UK Top 40, winning a Grammy Award for Best Male Pop Vocal Performance. Reviews for *Pilgrim*, Clapton's first album of original material since 1989's *Journeyman*, were mixed. Despite a checkered private life that, as well as multiple relationships, has also included spells of alcohol and substance abuse, Clapton has continued to make music. Considered one of the greatest guitarists of all time, Eric has left a multifaceted musical legacy.

In 1991, Conor fell to his death from a 53rd-floor apartment. He was only four years old. The loss of the boy, and with him Eric's only sense of connection with his father, sent the guitarist into a deep depression. As ever, he turned to his music to dull the pain. The first result of this therapy was the song "Tears in Heaven," a worldwide hit in 1992. Another song, "My Father's Eyes," also explored the feelings that Clapton might experience if he met his father in heaven.

How will I know him
When I look in my
father's eyes?

Clapton occasionally performed the song in various forms between then and 1998 when a new version became another hit for him. He hasn't played "My Father's Eyes" or "Tears in Heaven," live since 2004. Time has healed the scars, and Clapton no longer feels the emotions he needed

The normally evasive gaze of Eric Clapton's eyes staring straight into camera during his time playing with Cream.

to feel in order to play either of the songs. "They're kind of gone," he says, "and I really don't want them to come back."

The release of the song prompted a Canadian journalist to investigate the story of Clapton's father. Delving into the life of the man, he traced a number of half brothers and sisters for Eric. He also found a photo of Eric's father, and in 1998 the guitarist was able, for the first time ever, to see his father's eyes. Clapton himself has four daughters but no other sons.

My Old Man
Joni Mitchell

In the late 1960s Laurel Canyon, near Los Angeles, was home to many of the key players of hippie counterculture. Stars like Jimi Hendrix and Carole King and members of bands including the Monkees and the Doors lived there. Joni Mitchell's house in the Canyon was a sort of unofficial clubhouse for folk-rock players from groups like the Byrds and Buffalo Springfield, and it was at a jam session there one night that Crosby, Stills and Nash—the giants of the genre—played and sang together for the first time.

Graham Nash, singer with British beat group the Hollies, had come to California in search of a solo career. Instead, he found his lifelong musical partners in David Crosby and Stephen Stills, and he fell head over heels in love with Joni Mitchell.

Nash moved into Joni's home, and the couple were said to light up any room into which they walked. The two singer-songwriters were without a doubt a love match, and the house on Lookout Mountain Road became a hive of creative activity. Nash was working on songs that would form the

Graham Nash was looking for a more traditional, domesticated relationship than Joni Mitchell felt she could ever fit into.

basis for the classic album *Déjà Vu,* and Mitchell was writing her second collection, *Clouds.* Mornings for the Mitchell-Nash household consisted of breakfast in a Ventura Boulevard deli followed, according to Graham, by a race to be first at the piano.

Despite their obvious love for each other, they wanted different lives together. By the end of 1969, with Mitchell already working on her third album, *Ladies of the Canyon,* it was over between them. The breakup took a great emotional toll on Mitchell and with *Canyon* proving her most successful release yet, she took time off to recover through painting, writing, and travel.

Stepping back from public life allowed her to draw a line under the affair. It also reinvigorated her songwriting, and she returned with what many regard as the greatest album of raw confessional songs ever released— 1971's *Blue.* It included her piano ballad "My Old Man," inspired by her relationship with Nash. It was the fondest of love songs, but confirmed their incompatibility in its chorus:

> We don't need no piece of paper from the City Hall
> Keeping us tied and true.

Graham Nash, it seems, *did* need it. He wed actress Susan Sennett in 1977, and they are still married.

JONI MITCHELL was born in 1943 in Fort McLeod, Alberta, Canada. She began playing piano, guitar, and ukulele at an early age, and music ran alongside her other great love, painting. Joni enjoyed early success as a songwriter in the mid-1960s as artists like Tom Rush, George Hamilton IV, Buffy Sainte-Marie, and Judy Collins popularized her songs. Her third album, *Ladies of the Canyon,* on which "Big Yellow Taxi" appeared, was released in April 1970, the month after Joni Mitchell won her first Grammy Award for Best Folk Performance. The album became an FM radio staple and, by that autumn, had earned Joni her first gold album for sales of over a half million copies. Perhaps the most famous track on it was "Woodstock," penned by her about the previous year's festival (though she hadn't actually attended!) that would be a hit in the hands of friends Crosby, Stills, Nash, and Young (who had).

Rolling in the Deep
Adele

British pop diva and Grammy award winner Adele Adkins burst onto the scene in 2008 with her debut album, *19*, named for her age when recording it. Adored by fans on both sides of the pond, it was her sophomore effort *21*, combined with her performance at the Brit Awards in early 2011, that really cemented her superstar status. *21* comprised 11 deeply personal tracks about a mystery man that stole and subsequently broke Adele's heart during the three years between the albums.

The lead single from *21*, "Rolling in the Deep," whetted the public's appetite and is perhaps one of the most personal tracks on the album, with Adele starting by laying her feelings of anger and regret on the line. The song tells the tale of a love lost, with Adele lamenting, "We could have had it all."

While the lyrics display a commanding tone, Adele later revealed that it was the "biggest deal in my entire life, to date" and that writing the album was an emotional if not cathartic experience. "It broke my heart when I wrote [*21*], so the fact that people are taking it to their hearts is like the best way to recover— because I'm still not fully recovered. It's going to take me ten years to recover, I think, from the way I feel about [it]," she later said.

Adele fell for her beau while touring and promoting *19*—"He was older, he was successful in his own right," she told MTV, "whereas my boyfriends before were my age and not really doing much."

Adele at the start of her phenomenal rise to fame in 2008.

She added that the relationship opened her eyes to much more than she had previously been interested in. "I was interested in going clubbing and getting drunk. He got me interested in film and literature and food and wine and traveling and politics and history, and those were things I was never, ever interested in."

The title of "Rolling in the Deep" was adapted from "roll deep," a popular London phrase meaning having someone to watch your back, as Adele told *Rolling Stone*: "That's how I felt. I thought that's what I was always going to have, and it ended up not being the case."

Penned by Adele with the aid of British songwriter, Paul Epworth, "Rolling in the Deep" hit #1 in the US, topping the charts in eight countries in total, though it narrowly missed out in the U.K.

Despite the success, the memories of a love lost remained with Adele. However, in September 2011, she revealed to an audience at a London show: "We're becoming friends again. It's alright, I know what I'm doing. Enough time has gone by. ... The album helped me get over splitting up with my boyfriend. It helped me forgive and I hope that he has forgiven himself."

Many fans would likely want to know the identity of Adele's mystery lover, if only to thank him for inspiring one of the most successful British songs of the decade.

ADELE was born Adele Adkins and grew up in South London where she and her single mother moved when she was 11. She graduated from the BRIT School for the Performing Arts and Technology in Croydon, where she was a contemporary of Leona Lewis, in 2006. When a friend posted a three-song demo (which Adele had produced for a class project) on the social networking site Myspace, it led to her first recording contract. She became the first recipient of the Brit Awards Critics' Choice in 2008 and wasted no time in justifying their faith. The awards and accolades have continued.

Rooms on Fire
Stevie Nicks

In 1987 Fleetwood Mac were enjoying something of a revival thanks to the release of the album *Tango in the Night*. The following year the band capitalized on its success with the release of *Greatest Hits*, and vocalist Stevie Nicks went into the studio to write and record her fourth solo album, *The Other Side of the Mirror*. During its recording she had a brief but intense affair with her producer, UK synthesizer wizard Rupert Hine.

Rupert Hine as he appeared on his 1983 album cover, **The Wildest Wish to Fly.**

Hine's name is probably not widely known to the public except for its connection to Nicks. He also had a minor novelty hit as a member of the band Quantum Jump with "The Lone Ranger" in 1979. But the dozen albums he has recorded himself as a bandleader or solo artist pale into insignificance beside the more than 120 on which he has taken production credits.

Artists whom he has propelled to the album charts include Bob Geldof, Howard Jones, Murray Head, and the Fixx. It was probably his work on two of Tina Turner's multimillion-selling albums, *Private Dancer* and *Break Every Rule*, that shortlisted Hine for the Nicks job. But at their first meeting, the partnership became immediately more than a business relationship. "The night I met Rupert Hine was a dangerous one," Nicks wrote. "There was a connection between us that everyone around us instantly picked up on."

The sparks clearly flew, and throughout the four-month recording period in a Dutch stately home, they conducted their affair. During it, "Rooms on Fire" was written and recorded. "It's about when you're in a crowded room and you see a kind of person and your heart goes, 'Wow!' The whole world seems to be ablaze at that particular moment," said Nicks in an interview. "Whenever Rupert walked into one of these old, dark castle rooms, the rooms were on fire."

But when, at the end of recording, they moved to Hine's English studio to mix the album, the fire went out. Rumors abound about the reasons for the end of Nicks's affair with Hine, a married man, and none of them reflect well on him. Did he offer drugs to Nicks, a recovering addict? Did his wife become pregnant? Hine has never discussed the affair publicly, and all that Nicks will say is that "something happened to him that simply made it impossible for us to ever be together again. … It had nothing to do with love."

Rupert Hine returned to production work, first with Tina Turner and subsequently on further albums with Geldof, Eleanor McEvoy, Suzanne Vega, and many others. But he had worked his magic on *The Other Side of the Mirror*. It was a Top 10 hit in both the US and the UK; and "Rooms on Fire," the lead single from it, fared almost as well.

The 1989 European tour in support of it was a blur for Nicks, who became increasingly dependent on a sedative prescribed, ironically, to relieve her addiction to cocaine. But the 1990s saw a detoxed Stevie Nicks resume her career with renewed vigor. She still tours regularly, although she hasn't performed "Rooms on Fire" since 1999.

STEVIE NICKS, born in Phoenix, Arizona, in 1948 but in many ways the archetypal blonde Californian, was the 1980s' most successful female solo artist. She used Fleetwood Mac as her springboard to fame, having first joined forces with singer-songwriter Lindsey Buckingham in 1973. Her stock in trade was portraying a woman as a heartbreaker or a victim of love, and her solo tracks, featuring her distinctive agonized wail, achieved as much success as those she gave to Fleetwood Mac. "Rooms on Fire" was her final hit of the decade, a #16 hit on both sides of the Atlantic. She continues to record and perform both solo and with Fleetwood Mac, and she released her first solo album in a decade, *In Your Dreams*, in 2011.

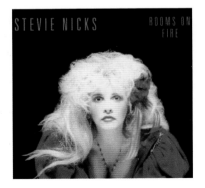

Rufus Is a Tit Man
Loudon Wainwright III

nterviews with Loudon Wainwright are rarely as insightful as simply listening to his songs. The man who Atlantic Records thought was going to be the "new Bob Dylan" was always going to have trouble working up a genuine rage against social injustice when he came from the privileged upbringing of Westchester County. His father, Loudon Wainwright Jr., was an editor for *Life* magazine in New York and the major arguments in the Wainwright household were about dodging the draft and getting busted for possession of marijuana.

Over a 40-year career, Loudon has chronicled and illuminated the arguments and events in his family in song with painful, 150-watt clarity. They may have started with attempts to rile his father, but they moved on to his wife and family. He married fellow folk singer Kate McGarrigle, and in 1973 Rufus was born, followed by Martha in 1976. All of them have songs. But while the songs he wrote about Martha—"Pretty Little Martha" and "Five Years Old"—were recorded after he split up with his wife in the mid-1970s and are permeated with a sense of melancholy for

LOUDON WAINWRIGHT III was one of many "new Dylans" to proliferate in the mid- to late 1960s. Wainwright stood out by leavening his earnest singer/ songwriter fare with wry humor, but this backfired when he had a surprise US hit single with "Dead Skunk." Labeled a novelty act and one-hit wonder, he happily resumed his low profile. He developed a parallel acting career, which began in the 1970s playing the "singing surgeon" on the TV show *M*A*S*H*, and has seen him play parts in movies *The Aviator, Big Fish, Elizabethtown, The 40-Year-Old Virgin,* and *Knocked Up.*

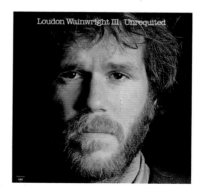

his absence through her childhood, his song for Rufus was written when the family were still together in New York. "Rufus Is a Tit Man" is written about his new-born son and it's played strictly for laughs.

> Come on mamma
> Come on and open up your
>   shirt
> Yeah you got the goods
>   mamma
> Give the little boy a squirt

Loudon sings about his jealousy for his son, sucking on something that's "sweeter than wine" and how by the way that Rufus burps it's "gotta taste fine." The glorious irony of the song was only revealed in the 1980s, when Rufus first told his parents he was gay and that in all honesty he was never going to be a tit man.

Since Rufus has grown up and developed his own career as a singer and composer, the friction that typified Loudon Wainwright III's relationship with his own father has continued across the generations.

Father and son. Loudon has also sung about his children's tendency to write a lot of their songs in "E."

Rufus's return song about his father has a lot less humor. "Dinner at Eight" from his third album, *Want One,* was inspired by an argument with LWIII at a restaurant. "We had just done a shoot for *Rolling Stone* together, and I told him he must be really happy that I had got him back in the magazine after all these years. That sort of kicked things off. Later in the evening he threatened to kill me. So I went home and wrote 'Dinner at Eight.'"

The family trait for turning autobiography into songs with deeply etched emotion has clearly passed from father to son.

Shine On You Crazy Diamond

Pink Floyd

In the last glimmering days of his solo career, Syd Barrett told veteran rock photographer Mick Rock, "I have a very irregular head," before retreating into a world of silence.

In the beginning Syd Barrett was Pink Floyd; he was the charismatic vocalist, the effervescent songwriter, the focus of the band. It was Syd who put together the names of veteran bluesmen Floyd Council and Pink

An early promotional shot of the just-signed-to-EMI Pink Floyd: (L–R) Roger Waters, Nick Mason, Syd Barrett, and Richard Wright.

Anderson to get the band's name; it was Syd who wrote the band's first two singles, "Arnold Layne" and "See Emily Play"; it was Syd who wrote eight of the eleven tracks on their first album, *The Piper at the Gates of Dawn,* and cowrote another two.

The band had emerged from the LSD-fueled psychedelic scene of the mid-1960s, playing extended progressive rock improvisations at deafening volumes at the UFO Club, all done to a psychedelic light show that allowed people to dance and have their minds blown.

The rigors of the pop business and the need to have three-minute singles and constantly promote their act didn't sit well with Syd. Their two hit singles were wildly different from their onstage repertoire, and Barrett would aggravate fans by sometimes refusing to play the songs they had come to hear.

While Pink Floyd were recording their debut album at Abbey Road, the Beatles were in the studio next door. Syd idolized John Lennon, who had made a stand against performing on mainstream pop programs, referring the group to make promotional films that could be shown instead. As the pressure grew on Pink Floyd following two successful singles, Syd wanted to opt out of the fame game. He had been indulged as the youngest son in a family of five and had indulged himself again in large quantities of LSD. He started to rebel against the role prescribed for him by his record company and the timetable it imposed on his creativity.

His behavior started getting more and more erratic. On the band's debut American tour in 1967, he refused to answer questions on Pat Boone's TV show and gave rude responses to Dick Clark on *American Bandstand.* At the band's gig at the Fillmore in San Francisco, Barrett slowly detuned his guitar through a performance of "Interstellar Overdrive," while at some gigs he would play one chord throughout or just stand there. The American tour was cut short.

In one final fling, their management sent the band out on the Jimi Hendrix tour in fall 1967, a "one night pop package" of seven bands headlined by the Jimi Hendrix Experience and including Amen Corner, the Move, and the Nice. On nights when Syd wasn't feeling like it, he would stay on the tour bus or wander off at the last minute, leaving the band to improvise or draft in Davy O'List from the Nice. "We staggered on thinking that we could manage without Syd, so we put up with what can only be described as a maniac," concluded drummer Nick Mason.

To cover Syd's absences and onstage antics, the band decided to draft in a friend, David Gilmour, to play live with them. They played five gigs as a five-piece before one day deciding to save themselves a lot of trouble by not picking Syd up. In early March 1968 bassist Roger Waters sat down with Syd and proposed he take the Brian Wilson option, to write and record with the band, but let the new four-piece play at gigs and do the promotional work.

"I thought I'd convinced him that it was a good idea but it didn't mean much because he was likely to totally change his mind about anything in an hour," Waters told Syd's biographers Mike Watkinson and Pete Anderson. Pink Floyd's managers certainly didn't think it was a good idea—their belief in the power of Syd was so strong that they agreed to part company with Waters and the rest of the band. They were convinced that they would achieve nothing without Barrett—it proved to be one of the costliest rock management decisions of all time.

The news that Syd had left the band came out on April 6, 1968, and though his management tried to get him into the studio to embark on solo work, they began to realize the difficulty of the task. Meanwhile Pink Floyd's career gained momentum with *A Saucerful of Secrets*, *Soundtrack for the film More*, *Ummagumma*, and *Atom Heart Mother*.

A high usage of LSD coupled with mental instability pushed Syd's erratic behavior to the limit. The fact that Pink Floyd were becoming more and more popular meant that sales of the first album were mounting,

PINK FLOYD evolved with the times, moving from 1960s psychedelia to a more progressive rock sound in the 1970s and 1980s. *The Dark Side of the Moon* established them in the global premier league of arena-fillers in 1973 and topped the US chart. Follow-up *Wish You Were Here* received mixed reviews on its late 1975 release. Bassist and covocalist Roger Waters left in 1985 after his working relationship with Gilmour finally foundered. The band reunited for Bob Geldof's Live 8 in 2005, but future reunions became unlikely after Richard Wright's death in 2008.

giving him a steady stream of royalties. He could sit in his apartment and do nothing. With the help of David Gilmour and latterly Roger Waters, they helped Syd fashion two solo albums of sketchily assembled material. *The Madcap Laughs* and then *Barrett* showed a few signs of his twinkling genius, but his star was fading and outtakes from the session show that Syd rarely played any track the same way from one take to the next.

In contrast, Roger Waters's writing star was ascending and the multi-platinum-selling *The Dark Side of the Moon*, with its reference to madness, hinted that the source of inspiration was close to home. For their follow-up album, *Wish You Were Here*, the band tackled the subject head on and devoted "Shine On You Crazy Diamond" to their former leader. Bizarrely, Syd turned up at the studio in 1975 while they were recording it. By this time he had put on weight and shaved off all of his hair. Keyboardist Richard Wright didn't even recognize him. "I saw this guy jumping up and down and brushing his teeth, and then somebody told me it was Syd." The band were shocked and the guilt that had riven them since his departure only intensified.

It was the last time they would see him. Syd withdrew to his mother's house in Cambridge and resisted all attempts to lure him back to the music business. After his mother's death he lived alone, frequently the target of Syd spotters and curious fans. He kept to himself as much as he could. News only resurfaced in 2006 when it was reported that he had fallen victim to pancreatic cancer.

By 1968 Syd had undergone a dark transformation. Childhood friend David Gilmour was shocked at the change.

Silver Springs
Fleetwood Mac

Anglo-American band Fleetwood Mac, formed in 1967, enjoyed a decade of success before rocketing to international stardom in 1977, less than three years after the arrival of new guitarist Lindsey Buckingham and vocalist Stevie Nicks. The band's 1977 album, *Rumours*, would top the US charts for more than six months, sell over 40 million copies, and become one of the Top Ten best-selling albums of all time.

The album was born from fractured interband relationships; bassist John McVie divorced his wife, vocalist Chrissie, while Nicks and Buckingham were embroiled in a tumultuous relationship. Nicks would later say of her and Lindsey: "He and I were about as compatible as a boa constrictor and a rat."

Though never officially hitched, Nicks and Buckingham were virtually inseparable, with Stevie once admitting: "We lived together for six years. I cooked for him. I did the laundry. I took care of him. It was as close to being married as I will ever be again."

But driving the band to greater heights extracted a price in the form of a broken relationship. Suddenly, a couple that had once been infatuated with each other could barely stand to be near each other. "Everything about me seemed to bug him."

"Silver Springs" is an intensely personal Nicks-penned track that displays her feelings in the wake of her split with Buckingham. So when the song was pulled from *Rumours* and relegated to a mere B-side without her knowledge, it hit her hard.

Lindsey and Stevie. Nicks was devastated when her track was left off **Rumours.**

"It was probably one of the most devastating things anybody has ever done to me in my life," she later recalled. "I remember vividly running out into the middle of the record plant studio parking lot and screaming, because I knew that 'Silver Springs' deserved to be on that record. [Lindsey] didn't write beautiful love songs about me, but I did write some beautiful love songs about him."

> I'll follow you down 'til the sound of my voice will haunt you
> You'll never get away from the sound of the woman that loves you

"Silver Springs" would eventually have its day in the sun. While its omission from *Rumours* was reported to be a factor in Nicks's quitting the band in 1991, it would ultimately be the track that helped reunite the band's most successful line-up in 1997. Nicks told MTV in 2009 that time does indeed heal wounds: "I don't feel like screaming at Lindsey right now. I'm not in a violent state of mind. I want people to leave feeling the emotion of 'Silver Springs,' but without seeing Lindsey and I clawing at each other."

She remains philosophical in her take on the events that inspired some of the band's biggest hits, as well as "Silver Springs": "They say that great art comes out of great tragedy."

FLEETWOOD MAC has always been a fluid entity. Frequent changes in members and music direction have helped the band remain popular throughout the years.

Rumours was their second album with new vocalist Stevie Nicks and, like their previous eponymous LP, had hit the top spot on the Billboard Hot 100. Although part of the album's recording sessions, B-side "Silver Springs" is familiar only to their fans.

Fleetwood Mac continued to release albums into the 21st century, despite many more alterations in personnel. The band's popularity endures.

Smile
Lily Allen

"**S**mile" was the UK #1 hit that brought Lily Allen to the attention first of her native Britain and, later, the world. The first single from her 2006 debut album, *Alright, Still*, would even be featured on the hit US drama-comedy *Glee* three years later. But laced throughout the upbeat melody, sampled from 1960s reggae band the Soul Brothers' "Free Soul," are bittersweet lyrics, born from a dark tale of rejection, hurt, and even depression, of which the world would later find out.

The track was inspired by her turbulent relationship and subsequent breakup with boyfriend DJ Lester Lloyd. Eighteen-year-old Lily began dating Lloyd and quickly fell head over heels, believing him to be "the love of my life." However, teenage first loves seldom endure and it wasn't long before the pair's relationship hit the rocks.

The lyrics explain the breakup from Lily's eyes, leaving nothing to the imagination:

> I was wanting more
> But you were fucking that girl next door

LILY ALLEN, daughter of British alternative comedian Keith Allen, shot to stardom on the social networking website Myspace, attracting a cult following through a series of videos and recordings.

Happily, after several false starts, she found the perfect man in painter and decorator Sam Cooper, whom she married in June 2011. She appeared to have turned her back on showbusiness after a second album, 2009's *It's Not Me, It's You*, in favor of running a fashion business with her sister Sarah, though changes of mind are very much part of her persona. She often uses Twitter to inform her fans of her ever-shifting intentions.

The breakup hit Lily hard and she spiraled into depression before checking into the Priory rehab clinic.

"It's a situation many girls will relate to," she told *The Sun* newspaper. "I was really young and in love. I fell to pieces, trying to make him take me back, trying to make it work. It was a horrible time. At the age of 17 and 18 all these emotions are coming through and it's hard to cope. I started to get depressed and anyone who suffers from depression knows that it can soon get so bad that you can't get out of bed."

It wasn't long before she produced her own album and the song was released, bringing Lloyd to the public's attention as the "inspiration" for the track. He sold his story to the UK newspaper the *Daily Mirror,* cashing in with tales of drug-fueled escapades and sex at her mother's council flat. But he denied ever cheating on Lily.

Allen onstage in 2006. No small bottle of Evian for Lily.

"I know she's telling everyone that I slept with her best friend, but it's rubbish. I don't even know which friend she means. She's a sweet girl and I loved her. I still think she's cool and we still talk. We just fell out of love. We're both still young and it was the first time either of us had been properly in love. Yeah, I suppose we are the loves of each other's lives and it was brilliant while it lasted."

Since then, Allen says that men have proved a lot more careful around her. "Now guys are really nice when they're breaking up with me because they don't want to end up on a song!" Candidates for the sexually lazy boyfriend in her single "Not Fair" ought to watch out.

Someone Saved My Life Tonight

Elton John

In 1975, Elton John released *Captain Fantastic and the Brown Dirt Cowboy*, an autobiographical album about the early days of his songwriting partnership with lyricist Bernie Taupin. "Someone Saved My Life Tonight" tells of how Taupin and Long John Baldry talked Elton out of a potentially disastrous marriage.

Taupin and John met in 1967 after answering a Liberty Records advertisement seeking new talent. Although both failed the audition, A&R man Ray Williams suggested they collaborate and Taupin relocated from rural Lincolnshire to London. The duo developed a somewhat unorthodox working method; Elton composed the music to Bernie's already completed lyrics, with little further discussion between them.

Nicknamed "Long John" because of his six-foot-seven-inch stature, vocalist Baldry was a fixture of London's early 1960s blues scene, playing with various members of the Rolling Stones and Rod Stewart. In 1966, after some personnel changes, Elton's group Bluesology became Baldry's backing band.

On Christmas Eve 1967, Elton John met Linda Woodrow in Sheffield at a gig with Baldry. Linda was the heiress to the Epicure Pickle company and lived off a comfortable trust fund. Soon afterward, they became engaged—notwithstanding the fact that Elton was gay—and moved into a north London flat with Taupin as their lodger. Marriage loomed ominously like a "slip noose" for Elton. "Altar-bound, hypnotized," his fate seemed inescapable.

On June 7, 1968, Elton, who'd gone solo on leaving Baldry's employ, had written to an old school friend. "Just a few lines to let you know I am getting married on 22nd June at Uxbridge Registry offices. … Well if you think it's a bit sudden you're right. Seeing as we were living together we thought we might as well get married. Nothing much happening record-wise because I've got problems with my record company at the moment."

Elton's summary of what happened next is fairly straightforward. "I went out and got drunk with Long John Baldry and Bernie and they said

Elton John and lyricist Bernie Taupin who "rescued" Elton from one of the least convincing suicide attempts of all time.

I shouldn't get married. I knew he was right but I didn't know how to get out of it, so I just got drunk and went home and said I'm not getting married."

The venue for this three-man meeting of minds was the Bag O'Nails club in London's fashionable Carnaby Street. The innocent Elton later admitted, "I cannot believe I never realized that Baldry was gay. I mean, I didn't realize I was gay at that time, but looking back on it now, John couldn't have been any more gay if he tried."

Bernie Taupin also recalls an almost laughable suicide attempt that had happened around a week before. "One day I was coming out of my room and, walking down the hall, I smelled gas. I thought, 'Oh, great, somebody's left the oven on in the kitchen.' I walked in the kitchen and there's Elton lying on the floor with the gas oven open. My immediate thought should have been 'Oh, my God, he's tried to kill himself!' But I started laughing because he'd got the gas oven open, he was lying on a pillow and he'd opened all the windows."

Elton clearly trusted his songwriting partner to speak for him through the lyrics of the song. Indeed, so adept was Taupin at it that the singer referred to

Someone Saved My Life Tonight | **107**

Veteran British blues singer Long John Baldry, who took Elton John down to the pub and told him, "Don't do it."

his 1974 single "The Bitch Is Back" as "kind of my theme song." Long John Baldry, he said, had reasoned that "you are more in love with Bernie than this woman [Linda]"—a fact Elton later acknowledged, calling Taupin "the brother I had always wanted."

Amazingly, having dodged marriage's "slip noose" once, Elton would actually tie the knot 16 years later. His bride was Renate Blauel, a German woman he met in AIR London Studios where she was working as a tape operator.

When the pair marched boldly up the aisle at St. Mark's Church in Darling Point, Sydney, on Valentine's Day 1984, there was a general air of astonishment. But Bernie, one of the best men along with manager John Reid, was not surprised, saying, "I always knew that if Elton suddenly got a bee in his bonnet about wanting a family, it was likely to happen pretty suddenly."

On the other side of the world, however, the *Sunday Mirror* was busily tracking down Linda Woodrow, the first woman to have set her sights on being Mrs. Elton John (or, more accurately, Mrs. Reg Dwight at that time). *The Sun* covered the wedding under the headline "Good On Yer, Poofter," allegedly a comment from a ribald Australian as the couple emerged from the church.

The new Mrs. John was by Elton's side in Wembley Stadium's royal box in May 1984 as the Watford's chairman enjoyed his club's FA Cup Final against Everton. Renate was also with Elton on his next recording date, engineering new release *Breaking Hearts*. But the Johns' marriage ended in divorce in 1988.

In a sad echo of Elton's early home life, when his father had been absent on national service, touring had left Renate living more or less alone in his Woodside, Berkshire, home for many months. Elton biographer Philip Norman suggests it was probably no coincidence that, when he and Renate finally split, he would dramatically divest himself of two full decades' worth of memorabilia, furnishings and *objets d'art* in an apparent attempt to draw a line under his life and start again from scratch—a single man and a simpler man.

The former status would change after Elton John met current partner, Canadian filmmaker David Furnish, in 1993. They entered into a civil partnership on December 21, 2005, the first day that civil partnerships could be performed in England, and have a son, Zachary Jackson Levon Furnish-John, born in 2010.

As for Linda Woodrow, now Linda Hannon, she now lives in the United States and has since married four times. Long John Baldry died of a severe chest infection in 2005, at age 64. Mainstream musical success had largely eluded him, with the exception of 1967 UK chart topper "Let the Heartaches Begin, "a ballad totally at odds with his bluesy musical leanings. He overcame mental problems in the 1970s, having been institutionalized for a while, to pursue a successful acting career with supporting parts in numerous films.

ELTON JOHN, born Reginald Dwight in 1947, began learning piano at four and later attended the Royal College of Music in London. After teaming up with Bernie Taupin, Elton recorded his debut album *Empty Sky* as a showcase for their material. *Captain Fantastic and the Brown Dirt Cowboy* was John's ninth album in six years. "Someone Saved My Life Tonight" was the only single taken from the album, reaching number 4 in the US. One of the world's most famous rock stars, Elton John's career has produced over 30 albums which have sold in excess of 250 million copies.

Song for Guy
Elton John

By the summer of 1978, Elton John hadn't had a Top 20 hit since "Sorry Seems to Be the Hardest Word" in November 1976. *Blue Moves*, the album from which "Sorry" was taken, was an uninspired affair, and during the tour to promote it Elton declared from the stage of Wembley Arena that it would be his last. After six extraordinary years at the top, he and his creative team (producer Gus Dudgeon and lyric writer Bernie Taupin) were burnt out.

He took a long break from touring and recording, and when he returned to the studio in January 1978 it was without Dudgeon and Taupin. His

Rocket Records boss Elton Hercules John, photographed in 1978.

new musical partners were the relatively unknown lyricist Gary Osborne and producer Clive Franks. Franks and Osborne had previously collaborated on hits for Kiki Dee, an early signing to Elton John's Rocket Records label.

Their arrival had the desired effect: the change shook up Elton's creative juices and delivered the 1978 album *A Single Man*, a cocktail of strong pop songs hailed as his best collection since *Captain Fantastic and the Brown Dirt Cowboy* in 1975. The energetic first single from it, "Part Time Love," duly returned Elton to the charts (#15 in the UK, #22 in the US).

The album took nine months to record and was released in October 1978 on Rocket Records, of course. Rocket had been formed by John, Taupin, Dudgeon, and others in 1972 (and named after their first hit that year, "Rocket Man"). It was a relatively small operation, and Elton personally knew everyone who worked for it. One who came into frequent contact with him was 17-year-old Guy Burchett, the company's motorcycle courier. Among Guy's duties were the collection and delivery of the precious tapes and masters during the long recording period.

One of the last tracks to be recorded for *A Single Man* (on August 18, 1978) was a reflective piece for solo piano. It's an instrumental, apart from the rather mournful repetition of the phrase, "Life ... isn't everything." As Elton John sat composing it, he recalls, "I imagined myself floating into space and looking down at my own body. I was imagining myself dying. Morbidly obsessed with these thoughts, I wrote this song about death."

The following day he learned that Guy had been killed in a motorcycle accident. Elton, greatly distressed at the loss of a well-liked colleague, named the melancholy recording after him.

The track closes the album. It did not get a single release in the US, where it was considered too similar to a recent piano-led instrumental hit by Frank Mills, "Music Box Dancer." But at the end of 1978 it gave Elton John his first UK Top Five hit since 1973. His lyricist Gary Osborne may have been less than delighted. As an instrumental it has none of his lyrics, and the B-side was "Lovesick," a previously unreleased collaboration by Elton with Gary's predecessor Bernie Taupin.

ELTON JOHN is one of the most successful singer-songwriters of all time. He had the biggest-selling single since UK and US singles charts when he rerecorded *Candle in the Wind* in memory of Princess Diana in 1997—the song sold over 35 million copies worldwide. The royalties went to charity, and Elton's own AIDS Foundation has raised over $200 million to support work in 55 countries. As well as lending his hand to musical soundtracks including Disney classic *The Lion King*, John spent the late 1990s and 2000s performing duets with contemporary artists such as 2Pac and the Killers.

Speechless
Lady Gaga

Famed for her outrageous clothes, makeup, and personality, onstage and offstage, many would be forgiven for thinking Lady Gaga would never write a ballad, let alone one about her father. But the entertainment phenomenon from New York born Stefani Germanotta did just that in late 2009.

Behind the ostentatious façade, Lady Gaga is simply a girl who loved her parents, and, unlike many performers, she had only fond memories of her childhood: "My parents were supportive of anything creative I wanted to do, whether it was playing piano or taking method acting classes. They liked that I was a motivated young person."

Joseph Germanotta had a history of heart problems, as Gaga later recalled: "I've known about my father's condition for about 15 years. He told me whatever happens, happens." It was this casual attitude toward his illness that prompted Gaga to pen "Speechless" in April 2009.

Lady Gaga followed by her father, the reluctant patient, Joseph Germanotta.

While on tour in Australia, Gaga received a call—Joseph's condition had worsened and he required heart surgery. "He was not gonna get the surgery. I was getting ready to lose my dad," she told a US radio station; "Speechless" was her plea to her father to get the help that would save his life. The lyrics tell of her disbelief at her father's reluctance to fight to the end.

Gaga halted her promotional tour and returned to New York to be with her parents, not only to lend her support but also to give her father a harsh reality check. "I said this is not just your heart, this is all of our hearts. If you go, I'm gonna quit music, Mom's not gonna be able to function. This is gonna affect all of us and you have to do it."

Joseph, whom she described in "Speechless" as having "James Dean glossy eyes … tight jeans … long hair … and cigarette stained lies," eventually agreed to the surgery for the sake of his family. Gaga put her newfound wealth to the best possible use, as she paid for the surgery out of her own pocket, sharing her joy with her millions of fans on the social network Twitter: "My Daddy had open-heart surgery today. And after long hours, and lots of tears, they healed his broken heart, and mine. Speechless."

Her father on the mend, Gaga was able to return to work and the road in time for *The Fame Monster*'s release in November 2009. She reflected on the ordeal after the event: "It was the biggest nightmare of my life. My father is my whole world; I'm such a daddy's girl."

No stranger to tattoos, Lady Gaga has one piece of body art on her shoulder that is particularly special to her, and a reminder of the man in her life that she nearly lost—the single word "Dad" inside a heart.

LADY GAGA is one of the entertainment icons of the current century. She mixed the appeal of Madonna and Michael Jackson with the glam-rock sensibilities of Bowie and Freddie Mercury to produce music and videos that captured a generation.

Trendsetting outfits, stage props, and hairstyles have kept her in the spotlight, notoriously one made of meat she wore at the 2010 MTV Video Awards.

Using video and social media to proclaim her message loudly and proudly, while espousing the causes of life's misfits, the former Stefani Germanotta looks set to rule the showbiz roost for some while to come.

Stuck in a Moment You Can't Get Out Of

U2

Imagine the scene—rural Provence on France's Côte d'Azur. The Mediterranean Sea twinkles in the sunlight. The frontmen of two of the world's most successful bands, Bono from U2 and INXS's Michael Hutchence, have villas nearby. When in residence, they hang out together. So, what do two rich, famous rock stars talk about amid this idyllic setting? According to Bono, "We discussed suicide a few times and we both agreed how pathetic it was." So the Irish rock star was more than staggered when he heard the news.

Michael Hutchence on the road in the UK with his band INXS in 1988. A punishing schedule, depression, and court battles proved too much in the end.

Hutchence's smoldering good looks meant that he was equally well-known for a series of highly publicized romances with Kylie Minogue, Danish supermodel Helena Christensen, and Bob Geldof's ex-wife, TV presenter and journalist Paula Yates. Since suffering a fractured skull in 1992, Hutchence had experienced bouts of depression. Custody battles over Geldof and Yates's children weighed heavily, as did the absence of his own daughter, Tiger Lily. INXS were on the final leg of a world tour when his body was found in a Sydney hotel room on November 22, 1997. He had committed suicide by hanging himself.

U2 were also on the road in America, flying between shows, when Bono heard the news. At first he didn't know how to react. "You always think if it's a mate that there was something you could have done."

Bono's eventual response was to write a song that took its title from a comment he made when interviewed on Australian television. When asked if he was angry with Hutchence, Bono replied that he wasn't because his friend was stuck in a moment that he couldn't get out of.

The Irish singer explained, "It's a row between mates. You're kinda trying to wake them up out of an idea. In my case it's a row I didn't have while he was alive. I feel the biggest respect I could pay to him was not to write some stupid soppy fucking song, so I wrote a really tough, nasty little number, slapping him around the head. And I'm sorry, but that's how it came out of me."

U2 often paid tribute to Michael Hutchence at gigs by playing INXS songs over the PA and dedicating "Stuck in a Moment" to him onstage. In 1999, Bono added his vocals to complete "Slide Away," a virtual duet with Hutchence that was included on the singer's posthumous solo LP.

Bono later confessed to feelings of guilt over what happened. "I felt I had let Michael down because I was lost in my own business and hadn't called as much as I would have liked."

As a tragic footnote, Paula Yates died of a heroin overdose in September 2000. Though many thought it was suicide, the coroner reported that it was a result of "foolish and incautious behavior."

U2 are unique in having the same four members throughout their lengthy existence. Formed in Dublin in 1977, they rose to become one of the biggest rock bands in the world. The anthemic "New Year's Day" gave them a debut hit in 1983 and the parent album *War* was a transatlantic success. U2's momentum built with 1984's *The Unforgettable Fire* and 1987's *The Joshua Tree*, which sold 25 million copies worldwide. The 1990s saw the band experiment by adding electronic influences to *Achtung Baby* followed by the even more ambitious *Zooropa*. The Grammy award–winning "Stuck in a Moment" was the second single from their ninth album, 2000's *All That You Can't Leave Behind*.

Tears in Heaven
Eric Clapton

Eric Clapton may have devoted two of his most memorable songs to fatherhood, but it was a role that he found difficult. He had been married to Pattie ("Layla," "Wonderful Tonight") Boyd for nine years when he started a relationship with Italian model Loredana "Lory" del Santo. By this stage in his life Clapton had beaten the demons of heroin addiction but found it much harder to kick the bottle, as did Boyd on occasions. The couple had tried unsuccessfully to start a family using IVF, and it was cited as one of the reasons the marriage was falling apart.

So when del Santo told Eric she wanted a baby, she says he was happy to agree. The intervening months between conception and birth were not easy, as she commuted back and forth between Milan and London, but she eventually gave birth to Conor in August 1986.

Clapton, who was still married to Pattie Boyd, dreamt up a far-fetched plan that he, Lory, Conor, and Patti could all live together in his Surrey mansion, but Boyd gave it short shrift and began divorce proceedings. Neither woman knew at the time that Clapton was already a father. He had embarked on a year-long affair with Yvonne Kelly, which had produced a daughter, Ruth, born in January 1985. Eric paid her maintenance but had managed to keep it a secret from his wife right up until the death of his son in 1991.

After Pattie moved out and Lory moved in, del Santo hoped they might establish a good family life and Eric could put some aspects of his rock 'n' roll lifestyle behind him. Speaking to *The Daily Mail's* Lisa Seward, she said, "But then it became obvious that he couldn't cope with our baby, and the idea that a baby's needs come first. For a start, there was no longer the silence he craved, and, as Conor grew bigger, Eric just couldn't handle the mess a child makes. He resented the presence of a baby in a life which had previously been so ordered and simple.

"He would never play with Conor. He would just look at him as if he was a world apart from him. Three years after Conor was born, I decided I couldn't wait any longer. I really wanted another baby and he was so insecure. We had to go our separate ways, just meeting up so he could see Conor from time to time. The tragedy is that the day he finally realised what Conor meant to him was just the day before our son died."

Eric Clapton with his son Conor in 1989. His partner Lory del Santo claimed that Clapton struggled with the noise and mess that a child brought to the house.

Tears in Heaven

After Lory and Clapton finally separated, Lory went to stay at a friend's apartment on New York's 57th street. The day before Conor died, Eric had visited them and taken his four-year-old son to the circus on Long Island. "When Eric got back he looked at me and said, 'I now understand what it means to have a child and be a father.' He was so happy."

The following day Eric was due to take Conor to Central Park Zoo, when the janitor arrived to do cleaning work on the windows of the 53rd-floor apartment. He had slid open a large glass window in one of the rooms. Conor ran in; he was playing hide and seek with his nanny. As the janitor tried to tell the nanny what he was doing with the window, Conor ran to the ledge in front of what was now an open space and fell through.

The funeral for Conor was held at St. Mary Magdelene's Church in the village of Ripley, Surrey, where Clapton lived. It was attended by celebrity friends including Phil Collins, George Harrison, and a supportive Pattie Boyd. Clapton's most public form of grieving came through the song

ERIC CLAPTON has made musical history with whomever he's played. He was an inductee to the Rock and Roll Hall of Fame as a solo artist as well as while a member of the Yardbirds and Cream—the only artist to achieve such a hat-trick. The creation of "Tears in Heaven" coincided with a period of his life when he consciously retreated from his "axe hero" past. In August 1990 his manager and two of his roadies (along with fellow musician Stevie Ray Vaughan) were killed in a helicopter accident while on tour. He took part in the MTV *Unplugged* series of acoustic shows and, in 1994, rediscovered his blues roots on the album *From the Cradle*, choosing to emulate his heroes by playing everything live without overdubs. In an interview, Clapton stated, "I almost subconsciously used music for myself as a healing agent, and lo and behold, it worked. ... I have got a great deal of happiness and a great deal of healing from music."

Lory del Santo with Conor. After his death she threw away all his clothes, as they were too painful a reminder. She has never listened to Clapton's song for the same reason.

"Tears in Heaven," and in 2004 he felt the process was over and stopped playing it.

Del Santo couldn't listen to it at all: "I had nightmares for years, when I heard my son's voice calling for help and I'd run to save him. Eric prays, but he's a very introspective person. To this day we have never ever spoken a word about what happened. We haven't even mentioned Conor's name. We don't need to because there are no words—we just both know. He wrote a song, 'Tears in Heaven,' about it which was his way of dealing with the grief, but I have never heard this song, nor do I ever want to." Once in Amsterdam she heard a radio DJ announce it and had to run outside to get away. She says that after his death she threw all Conor's toys and clothes away because it was too agonizing to see them at home.

Since those painful times del Santo has married and had sons Devin and Loren. She says she has tried hard not to look for the ghost of Conor in them both, even though Loren looks uncannily like Conor.

Eric remarried and with his wife, Melia, has three more daughters, Julie Rose (born June 2001), Ella Mae (born January 2003), and Sophie (born February 2005).

Thorn in My Side
Eurythmics

In March 1984 Eurythmics singer Annie Lennox married Radha Raman, a German Hare Krishna devotee. They had only known each other for a matter of weeks before tying the knot. The relationship lasted barely a year before they separated in February 1985. The song "Thorn in My Side" "came out of the breakup with my ex-husband," Lennox said.

> A bundle of lies
> You know that's all that it was worth

Before Raman, the statuesque, Scots-born Lennox had been romantically involved with fellow Eurythmic Dave Stewart. The pair first met in 1976 when Lennox was a waitress at a restaurant Stewart visited. Lennox recalled, "The first words Dave said were, 'Will you marry me?' I thought he was a serious nutter. But from that night on we were inseparable."

The lovers soon put together a band, the Catch, which evolved into the Tourists. After some minor success the Tourists fell apart, and electro-pop duo Eurythmics rose from its ashes in 1980. Stewart and Lennox were no longer an item, but their musical relationship flourished. As Stewart noted, "Most couples get famous and then break up. But we broke up and then got famous."

The split with Stewart cast a long shadow over Lennox. "I wasn't happy for years afterwards. I was always looking for a good relationship and you can see it in the songs, all this unrequited love. I was never in one spot, so my emotions were in turmoil.

Dave Stewart and Annie Lennox performing on the Revenge tour.

I never really enjoyed it—I should have settled down. Eurythmics was the mainstay of my existence and yet it was hollow. The irony is that though I was lonely, miserable and unsatisfied, it's a fantastic source for songs."

> I should have known better
> But I got what I deserved

"Part of the reason for jumping into [marriage] so quickly was a sense of longing for some form around my life. Thinking I could buy an instant marriage off the shelf like that ... [Dave] was opposed to the marriage and absolutely right to be opposed to it. ... But it was my statement to him that 'you can't tell me what to do with my life any more.' I had to say to him. 'I'm not your little girl. Let me make this mistake.'" Stewart recalled that, "Annie was channelling her anger and was so focused when she opened her mouth and delivered her cutting lyrics ... it was icy cold yet burning with passion."

After his brush with notoriety as Annie Lennox's husband, Radha Raman returned to the anonymous life of a Krishna follower. From 1988 to 2000 Lennox was married to Israeli film and record producer Uri Fruchtmann, with whom she had two daughters.

EURYTHMICS, named after a style of Greek dance, did not enjoy immediate success; their first album, *In the Garden,* made little impact. The title track of their second album *Sweet Dreams (Are Made of This)* was an American chart topper in 1983. Further international success followed with the albums *Touch* and *Be Yourself Tonight.* The second single from fourth album *Revenge,* "Thorn in My Side," gave them another British Top Five hit in 1986.

Lennox and Stewart's collaboration ended in 1990 after which they both pursued solo ventures. They reunited briefly in 1999 to record one more Eurythmics album, *Peace.'*

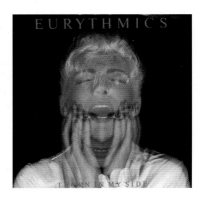

Underneath It All
No Doubt

"Underneath It All" is a love song. It doesn't exactly fit the traditional role of a ballad, but No Doubt weren't a conventional band. The Californian group enjoyed great success with their brand of alternative ska-infused pop rock, but their love for music from across the world meant that no two albums sounded the same. It was from this ethos and penchant for experimentation that one of their biggest hits stemmed.

No Doubt frontwoman Gwen Stefani was always the shining light in the band, as a successful solo career during the band's hiatus in 2004 confirmed. And her relationship with Gavin Rossdale, lead singer of British rock band Bush, made them one of the most popular celebrity couples of the early 2000s.

Gwen Stefani of No Doubt and Gavin Rossdale of British rock band Bush have maintained one of the longest-running relationships in rock.

The pair met in 1995 when No Doubt were recruited to open for Bush on a tour as breakout single "Just a Girl" was climbing the charts; the Goo Goo Dolls were also on the bill and became the couple's favorite band. They would soon embark on a relationship, despite living eight time zones apart, and this would prove as unconventional as anything they had done in their musical lives.

It appeared that Rossdale would not immediately commit to living together. "The thing is," Stefani confessed in a 2001 interview, "we still don't really live together. He lives there [London] and I live here [Los Angeles] and he's been staying here for three months because he's doing a record. It's been perfect because we got to really spend time together for the first time and we've been going out for five and a half years." The pair's volatile relationship even resulted in Stefani dying her hair pink after a fight had caused them to "break up for an hour"; she kept the color for a year.

Their courtship would become more conventional over time and result in marriage and two children, but it would also prove a bumpy ride due to Rossdale's checkered past. Gwen's budding relationship with the Bush frontman had already inspired her to write "New," one of the first songs written after the release of No Doubt's multiplatinum breakthrough album, *Tragic Kingdom.*

But it is "Underneath It All" that best encapsulates the pair's enduring friendship. It was written in London (where Stefani had traveled to meet her boyfriend) in just ten minutes by Stefani and British singer-producer Dave Stewart of Eurythmics fame, and was created with the help of backward string samples. The track's chorus was lifted from a journal entry written by Stefani after a day out with her man. "You're really lovely, underneath it all," she said, giving a brief glimpse into the dynamic of their relationship.

"The day before we went over there I was in the park with Gavin, and I had been keeping a journal," she told *Rolling Stone.* "And we were so in love, and I wrote that line, 'You're lovely underneath it all.' You know, like, 'After all the shit we've been through, you're a really good person. I really think I might like you.'"

The track is featured on No Doubt's fifth studio album, *Rock Steady,* and displays heavy Jamaican influences, as the band recorded the album in that country. A cameo role for dancehall legend Lady Saw, recruited at the suggestion of producers Sly Dunbar and Robbie Shakespeare, only added to the vibe.

"Underneath It All" charted at #3 in the US on its release in August 2002. It won a Grammy Award and went on to be featured in the film *50 First Dates* (2004).

Gwen and Gavin married in September 2002 at St. Paul's Church in London's Covent Garden. A second ceremony was held in Los Angeles two weeks later. According to Stefani, this was so that she had the opportunity to wear her custom-designed wedding dress by John Galliano twice. They then retreated to their private life on the West Coast.

At the same time, Rossdale split from Bush. He'd interspersed musical pursuits with acting through the decade (he'd made his screen debut the year before in the movie *Zoolander*) but had to wait until 2008 to enjoy his first solo hit with the single "Love Remains the Same."

A storm hit the pair two years into their marriage when a paternity test revealed Rossdale was the father of British model Daisy Lowe; he had enjoyed a relationship with her mother, Pearl, in the late 1980s. Gwen was reported to be "devastated" at the news, despite Daisy's conception occurring in early 1989, over half a decade before he embarked on their relationship.

Gwen revealed to *Rolling Stone* magazine in 2002 that they, like millions of other couples, still had fears and anxieties about the relationship: "It doesn't matter who you are—if I worked in the same McDonald's as Gavin, and he worked at the fryer, there are going to be trust issues.

NO DOUBT peaked with hit singles such as "Just a Girl" and the 1995 transatlantic #1 smash hit, "Don't Speak," from their third album *Tragic Kingdom*. They owed much of their success to Californian singer and songwriter Gwen Stefani. Stefani's solo career was always in the cards. She worked with dance and hip-hop producers such as Dr. Dre and the ever-popular Neptunes, and the plan worked. Her debut, 2004's *Love Angel Music Baby*, initially outsold any No Doubt album and contained the US #1 single "Hollaback Girl." At the time of writing, her solo career and that of No Doubt continue in tandem.

The couple married in London and Los Angeles so Gwen could wear her John Galliano wedding dress twice. They are seen here at the post-Oscars **Vanity Fair** *party in 2005.*

Is he flirting with the girl behind the French fries?" Resilient, Gwen and Gavin worked through their issues behind closed doors, as was the nature of their relationship. And they appeared to be back on track in 2006 when Stefani gave birth to their first son, Kingston; a second child, Zuma, arrived in 2008.

Though they seemingly weathered the storm of Rossdale's fatherhood (he broke off contact with the Lowes, and he now enjoys "a respectful friendship" with his daughter), more media attention came in 2010 when he finally admitted to a gay affair with cross-dressing pop star Marilyn in the 1980s when he was just 17 years old. Gavin had not admitted to the affair until then because of the media "glare" when Bush were first forging a career in the United States. "It's a part of growing up—that's it, no more, no less," he said.

But Stefani and Rossdale were bulletproof. Gwen told *Elle* magazine of her pride that she and Gavin had gone the distance. "I've been with Gavin for 14 years and, let's face it, that is a huge accomplishment. I feel so proud of that—it hasn't been the easiest journey." In a world where couples in the public eye can be ripped apart by tabloid rumors and gossip, it was clear that underneath it all, the pair had a stronger bond than most and were right for each other.

Walk on the Wild Side
Lou Reed

In the early years of the 1970s, Lou Reed was far more influential a figure than he was a commercial success. Steve Harley, Mott the Hoople (who covered his "Sweet Jane"), Jonathan Richman, and especially David Bowie were among those who had lent an ear and recycled what they heard. But this was clearly of little value to record label RCA, who were understandably more interested in selling records. So they teamed him with Bowie and his guitarist Mick Ronson, put the trio in Trident Studios, London, and waited expectantly for the results. Even they, however, must have been impressed at the performance of LP *Transformer* on its release in November 1972. It made #29 in the US and #13 in the glam-obsessed UK. It was propelled there by the single "Walk on the Wild Side."

Reed had been playing with "Wild Side" over a year before he recorded it; he had been asked to score a stage show of the 1956 novel by Nelson Algren of the same name. The play never happened, but Reed rewrote the original lyrics and came up with the song for which he is most likely to be remembered.

The fact that the song received radio airplay at all was, in retrospect, surprising. The notoriously conservative BBC clearly did not understand phrases like "giving head," so when Radio 1 DJ Tony Blackburn made the song his Record of the Week, its ascent to #10 was hampered by no censorship whatsoever. In the US, RCA took the precaution of issuing radio stations with a cleaned-up version of the song that also replaced the phrase "And the colored girls say" with "And the girls all say." Depending on the regional US market, the song was considered slightly politically incorrect, but DJs tended to play the unexpurgated version regardless.

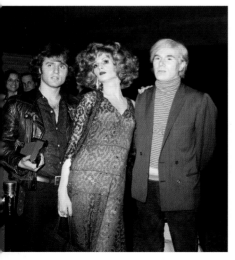

Gerard Malanga and Candy Darling with mentor and friend Andy Warhol.

Holly Woodlawn came from Miami, Florida, to star in Andy Warhol's 1970 movie **Trash.** *The transgendered actress took her name from the heroine of* **Breakfast at Tiffany's.**

Unlike Reed's underperforming solo debut, it contained mostly new material that post-dated the Velvet Underground. "Wild Side" was a story song with a cast of characters that all came from the Andy Warhol Factory scene. "Little Joe" refers to Joe Dallesandro, who was in several films by Warhol. "Sugar Plum Fairy" is the nickname of actor Joe Campbell, while "Holly," "Candy," and "Jackie" are based on Holly Woodlawn, Candy Darling, and Jackie Curtis, all real-life drag queens who appeared in Warhol's 1972 movie *Women in Revolt.*

Reed discussed the subjects' proclivities in a matter-of-fact monotone: Candy "in the back room ... was everybody's darling," Holly "shaved her legs and then he was a she," Little Joe "never once gave it away," Jackie "thought she was James Dean," and the Sugar Plum Fairy was "looking for soul food and a place to eat." He also refers to speed and valium, drug references that escaped the censor.

But it was the reaction of the characters involved that he feared. "I thought they would all claw my eyes out when I got back to New York," the singer later admitted. "Instead, Candy Darling told me he'd memorized all the songs and wanted to make a 'Candy Darling Sings Lou Reed' album. It probably wouldn't sell more than a hundred copies!"

Jackie Curtis ("Jackie is just speeding away/ Thought she was James Dean for a day"). Reed wasn't referring to a Coupé GT.

It was not the first time Reed had written a song mentioning Darling. "Candy Says" opened the third Velvet Underground album but did not attract anything like the attention "Wild Side" got. (It's also rumored that the Kinks' "Lola" was inspired by Darling.)

The musical hook of "Wild Side," audible from the outset, was a sliding bass line devised and played by session musician Herbie Flowers on an upright double-bass doubled by an electric bass. Flowers was modest about his contribution to the album. He once told *Mojo* writer Phil Sutcliffe, "You do the job and get your arse away. You take a £12 fee, you can't play a load of bollocks. Wouldn't it be awful if someone came up to me on the street and congratulated me for *Transformer*?" In fact, he was paid £17 for his work doubling instruments on the same track, apparently his motivation for suggesting the arrangement.

The saxophone solo was played not by Bowie, as many assumed, but by jazz musician Ronnie Ross, who had tutored a 12-year-old Bowie. Bowie booked Ross for the session but didn't tell him he'd be there. After Ross nailed the solo in one take, Bowie showed up to surprise his former sax teacher.

Mick Ronson credits his production and arrangement teaming with Bowie as "pretty sharp," and this was reflected in the speed at which the project was completed. "Records were done very quickly back then. I mean, when David and I produced Lou Reed's *Transformer*, we recorded the whole thing in 10 days, six hours a day. We recorded the whole thing in 60 hours and it was mixed and that was it."

Reed, for his part, admitted that he could very rarely understand a word Ronson said. "He had a thick Hull accent, and he'd have to repeat things five times! But he was a real sweet guy, and a great guitar player."

A public argument between Bowie and Reed ended their working relationship though the pair reconciled years later. But the song has continued to enjoy a life of its own. U2's Bono took it to a new worldwide audience in 1985 when he ad-libbed parts of the lyrics at Live Aid.

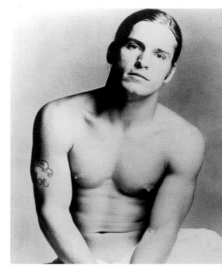

Joe Dallesandro ("Little Joe never once gave it away"). Dallesandro's denim-clad crotch famously graced the cover of the Rolling Stones' album Sticky Fingers.

LOU REED followed *Transformer* with *Berlin*, an album about two junkies in love that couldn't have been further from glam rock. He then toured the world with a heavy metal backing band, trashing his Velvet Underground standards before releasing *Metal Machine Music*, a double album of electronically generated audio feedback.

Reed has been romantically linked to musician and multimedia performance artist Laurie Anderson since the late 1990s. In 2011 he surprised his fans by announcing a collaborative album with heavy metal supergroup Metallica.

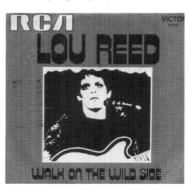

We Three
Patti Smith

"We Three" captures a moment in time in the summer of 1970 when three future giants of the New York art scene lived and loved together in the city's Chelsea Hotel. Patti Smith, Robert Mapplethorpe, and Jim Carroll fell into friendship by accident but grew side by side as artists. The three urged each other to new creative heights so successfully that by the end of the decade all three were icons in their own artistic fields.

Jim Carroll was a junkie poet who supplemented his income as a gay prostitute.

Patti, raised in poverty in New Jersey, trained as a teacher in the 1960s. But after an unwanted pregnancy (her daughter was put up for adoption), she drifted into New York in 1967. There she met a charismatic young graphic artist, Robert Mapplethorpe. They moved into an apartment in Brooklyn together and began an intense affair. "We fulfilled a role for each other," says Smith. "We woke up knowing we were no longer alone."

In 1969 Mapplethorpe dropped out of art college, and the couple moved to the Chelsea Hotel, a long-established artistic commune frequented by the great and the good of alternative culture. Mark Twain lived there; Dylan Thomas died there; Arthur C. Clarke wrote *2001: A Space Odyssey* there; and Nancy Spungen, girlfriend of Sid Vicious of the Sex Pistols, was found stabbed there in 1978.

Patti and Robert fit right in, she writing poetry, he working on collages. Mapplethorpe, struggling with his sexuality, began to realize in 1970 that he was gay. Smith then began a relationship with their mutual friend Jim Carroll, a junkie poet who supplemented his income (as Mapplethorpe did) as a gay prostitute. The three formed a powerful creative and sexual triangle, supporting each other's artistic endeavors and encouraging each other to break new boundaries.

Oh, can't you see that time
is the key
That will unlock the destiny
of we three?

Patti Smith helped to encourage Robert Mapplethorpe's photographic career.

Urged on by Mapplethorpe, Smith made her first forays into public performance at open poetry readings run by Carroll. Later Patti encouraged Jim to marry poetry and rock music, as she had since 1974 with guitarist Lenny Kaye—Jim made his musical debut supporting the Patti Smith Group in 1978. And according to Patti Smith, it was she who first encouraged Mapplethorpe in the mid-1970s to take up photography, the medium for which he is now best known.

Robert Mapplethorpe died in 1989 of an AIDS-related illness. His homoerotic, sadomasochistic photographs made him famous, and his portraits of Patti Smith grace many of her album covers. Jim Carroll, a college-sports star before drugs and poetry changed his direction, published his teenage journals as *The Basketball Diaries* in 1978. Carroll himself survived what Smith called "a slightly dangerous lifestyle" but passed away in 2010 at the age of 60.

Patti's career as punk poet continues, and she still performs "We Three" more than four decades after the period in her life that inspired it.

PATTI SMITH made waves with her 1975 LP, *Horses*, produced by John Cale. "We Three" appeared on her third album, *Easter* (1978). The album owed its success to the hit single "Because the Night," an unreleased Bruce Springsteen song she modified. After a break from the music industry, she returned to live performance in 1994 and has since recorded and toured relatively prolifically.

William, It Was Really Nothing

The Smiths

Clocking in at just two minutes ten seconds, "William, It Was Really Nothing" is propelled by Johnny Marr's Spanish guitar riff over which Morrissey intones a lyric that, like so many of his words, was rigorously analyzed by devotees. Who exactly *was* William?

A few months before the single's release in August 1984, Morrissey had spent some time with Billy Mackenzie, singer with Scottish band the Associates. The music-industry rumor mill was abuzz with speculation that Mackenzie had a crush on the Smiths' vocalist and even that the two were having an affair. Notoriously protective of his private life and silent about his sexuality, Morrissey claimed to be celibate, claiming to "never [have] been terribly interested in sex."

Morrissey described Mackenzie's visit to his London flat. "I found meeting Billy Mackenzie was very erratic, quite indescribable. He was like a whirlwind. He simply swept into the place and he seemed to be instantly all over the room. It was a fascinating study but one, I think, that would make me dizzy if it happened too often."

The Associates frontman committed a faux pas. "He walked off with one of my James Dean books, which is a persistent cause of anxiety to me ... Billy has got this sense of uncontrollable mischief, though I think that's exactly how he wants to be seen." Ultimately, according to Morrissey, the encounter ended in disappointment.

The Associates in 1982: Alan Rankine and Billy Mackenzie (standing).

"We spent hours searching for some common ground but I don't believe there was any."

The title, "William, It Was Really Nothing," is the most obvious reference to Mackenzie, although the song also hints at a regret that things didn't work out. In 1988, Mackenzie commented playfully on his relationship with Morrissey. "Oh, Morrissey's not celibate. I don't think Morrissey knows what celibacy is."

Billy Mackenzie's soaring, almost operatic falsetto was instantly recognizable. He and guitarist Alan Rankine became the Associates in 1979. After a pair of acclaimed independent albums, they scored a UK Top 10 hit with "Party Fears Two" from their major-label debut *Sulk* in 1982. The Associates looked set for further success, but Rankine left the band later that year.

Mackenzie and Rankine reunited in 1993, but the demos they recorded were not released until 2000. Their LP *Double Hipness* contained what appears to be a long-delayed response song, "Steven, You Were Really Something." But the title misspells Morrissey's rarely used first name (Stephen) and was written not by Mackenzie but by Rankine.

Suffering from clinical depression, Mackenzie committed suicide by taking an overdose of painkillers in January 1997. Morrissey paid a sincere tribute: "He was such a lovely person, and I feel very, very sad."

THE SMITHS came together in Manchester in 1982. "William, It Was Really Nothing" was their fifth single and third UK Top 20 hit.

The Smiths were one of the first bands to take British independent rock into the mainstream and the singles charts on a regular basis. The band's third, noncompilation, studio album, *The Queen Is Dead*, regularly appears in lists of the greatest ever made. Their prolific and massively influential career ended in 1987. Morrissey went on to pursue an eventful solo career.

His first solo single, "Suedehead," is also rumored to be about Billy Mackenzie.

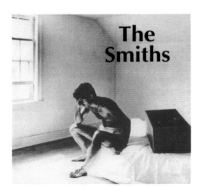

The Smiths

You Oughta Know
Alanis Morissette

Canadian singer Morissette hit the headlines with her third album, *Jagged Little Pill*—specifically the second track "You Oughta Know." It reveals in its very first verse how she performed oral sex on her boyfriend in a movie theater only to be dumped soon afterward, leaving her a woman scorned. After witnessing the ex-boyfriend proudly parading his new flame, Alanis challenged them both in a restaurant and demanded: "It was a slap in the face how quickly I was replaced/And are you thinking of me when you fuck her?"

Many critics accused Morissette of sensationalism, but she swears that it really happened. "I did do that, it's true," she shrugged. "I was a little worried about putting that incident into a song, but I don't believe in censoring anything, so I used it. It was something I had to do, this whole album came from a place inside of me. But it all boils down to the fact that I want to walk through life, not get dragged through it." "You Oughta Know" is a remarkably honest piece of lyricism, providing a useful warning for the average male: "Every time I scratch my nails down someone else's back/I hope you feel it."

Actor David Coulier is one of the many names in the frame for the guy in "You Oughta Know." Matt LeBlanc is another.

The song reached number 6 on the Billboard Hot 100, becoming her first Top 10 hit in the United States. The song inspired much press speculation as to the individual who had inspired it. These included actor Matt LeBlanc, who appeared in the video for Morissette's single "Walk Away" in 1991; Leslie Howe, the producer of Morissette's first two albums; and ice-hockey player Mike Peluso, who played for the Ottawa Senators. It was discussed in an episode of TV's *Curb Your Enthusiasm* on which Alanis guest starred, and the mystery surrounding the song brought comparisons to Carly Simon's 1972 song "You're So Vain."

But while Alanis, like Simon, remained coy, actor David Coulier, who played Joey Gladstone in the ABC sitcom *Full House*, appeared to put himself in the frame. "The Alanis I know is really fun to be around and really thoughtful and sweet. I think there's a lot of things in *Jagged Little Pill* that are very deep and fueled by her interactions with a lot of people. At the time we were dating, she was writing a lot of music, and I was a newly divorced, single father with a two-year-old son.

"She was living in Ottawa, Canada and I was living in Los Angeles. It was a tough time for me and a lot of distance for a budding relationship. I'll always think of her as a really great person. As far as being the so-called subject of 'You Oughta Know' ... I'll just let the urban legend folks keep spinning on that one."

Nor was its writer giving anything away. In a different interview a decade after release, Alanis justified her silence: "I've never talked about who my songs were about and I won't, because when I write them they're written for the sake of personal expression."

"You Oughta Know" won two Grammys, for Best Rock Song and Best Female Rock Vocal Performance, at the Grammy Awards of 1996. The song enjoyed an unlikely live cover by Britney Spears, Beyoncé sampled it during her "If I Were A Boy" performance on her 2009 I Am ... Tour, and Morissette herself performed it on the season nine finale of *American Idol* with finalist Crystal Bowersox.

ALANIS MORISSETTE, born in 1974, will forever be defined by her first internationally available album, 1995's *Jagged Little Pill*, which won her four Grammies and spawned seven major UK and US hits. It was clear that such overnight success would be hard if not impossible to follow up, and so it proved. By 2006 she had morphed into a TV star. Morissette left Madonna's Maverick Records label after her seventh studio album, *Flavors of Entanglement,* in 2008. Two years later she married rapper Mario **"MC Souleye" Treadway, becoming a mother in December 2010.**

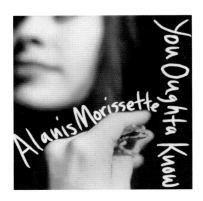

You're So Vain
Carly Simon

The identity of the target of Carly Simon's song "You're So Vain" has been the subject of intense speculation since its release in 1972. Several candidates have been put forward, including record-company mogul David Geffen.

Geffen was the head of Asylum Records in 1972, when it merged with Simon's label Elektra. She is thought to have been aggrieved by the attention Geffen was paying to the career of rival artist Joni Mitchell, a close friend of his, and wrote the song as an attack on him. Geffen fits the description of the flamboyant character: "You walked into the party/Like you were walking into a yacht."

Would former record-company boss David Geffen—seen here with Cher—have gone for a scarf that was apricot?

Featuring a sharply detailed portrait of its subject and the mocking refrain "You're so vain, you probably think this song is about you," "You're So Vain" exerts a perennial fascination. Simon has fielded countless questions about her inspiration. When the single came out, she was married to singer-songwriter James Taylor and maintained, "It's definitely not about James," while adding, "I can't possibly tell who it's about because it wouldn't be fair." Before her marriage, Simon had affairs with some high-profile stars, including Mick Jagger, who sings backing vocals on the song. Her comments on the rumor that Jagger was the inspiration for the song did not necessarily rule him out: "A lot of people think it's about Mick Jagger and that I have fooled him into actually singing on it, that I pulled that ruse."

Another former lover was film star Warren Beatty, and in 1983, she gave what appeared to be the strongest hint so far: "It certainly sounds like it was about Warren

Beatty. He certainly thought it was about him—he called me and said thanks for the song." Furthermore, she has claimed that the wearer of the famous apricot scarf was actor Nick Nolte but that the rest of the lyric was not about him.

David Geffen publicly acknowledged that he was gay in 1992, yet he had enjoyed relationships with women as a younger man. He almost married Cher in the 1970s and made enough of an impression on former housemate Joni Mitchell to have her write "Free Man in Paris" about him. The rumor that he was the inspiration for Simon's song was

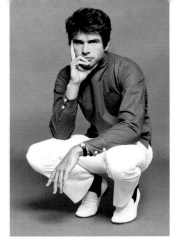

Warren Beatty liked the song and did indeed think it was about him.

fueled by her rerecording of it in 2009. The theory goes that she whispers "David," which can be heard when the song is played backwards. Naturally, Simon has denied this.

Acknowledging that it is not in her interests to provide a definitive answer to the question, Simon said, "I could never really solve it because, if I did, then no one would have anything to talk to me about."

CARLY SIMON's self-titled debut solo album was 1971's *Carly Simon,* which yielded her first US Top Ten single "That's the Way I've Always Heard It Should Be." "You're So Vain" from *No Secrets* has become her signature song. After "Nobody Does It Better," her theme tune to the Bond movie *The Spy Who Loved Me,* Simon's career fluctuated in the 1980s as she dabbled in jazz. The title track of her 1986 album *Coming Around Again* restored her to the charts. She has also enjoyed hits with the Chic-produced "Why" and as the uncredited vocalist on Will Powers's 1983 hit "Kissing with Confidence."

You've Got a Friend

Carole King

The question of whether "You've Got a Friend" was written about James Taylor remains. "It was not written for James," claimed Carole King, seeming definitive, in one interview. "It was one of those moments when I sat down at the piano and it wrote itself from some place other than me."

Maybe the reason she denied the fact was that she felt the press would try to link them romantically. After all, James Taylor, the man who took the song to US #1 in July 1971 for a single week, was one of those glamorous stars who slept with other stars in the close-knit West Coast scene; he dated Joni Mitchell, among others, and would woo and eventually wed another singer-songwriter, Carly Simon.

Also, King's relationship with Taylor was different than most of those she'd forged during more than a decade as a songwriter for hire. While she'd become an expert in providing the bullets for others to hit the chart target with, Taylor wrote his own material and was totally self-contained. It was a model she wanted to follow and would follow to multiplatinum effect with her 1971 album, *Tapestry*. Indeed, she was in the middle of recording this with producer Lou Adler as Taylor, with his producer Peter Asher, was ensconced in a studio just a few New York blocks away.

Why did Taylor record this song when he had so many of his own? That is also a point of debate, but with King electing to release "It's Too Late"/"I Feel the Earth Move" as the first double A-side single for the album—and scoring a US chart topper with it—he probably saw the overlooked song's potential. Ironically, it would be Taylor's only #1, but combined with a cover story in March 1971's *Time* magazine, it helped give his career the lift he craved.

Carole and James had been brought together by Danny "Kootch" Kortchmar, a childhood friend of Taylor's who, after accompanying him in his first band, the Flying Machine, played in a short-lived band called the City with King. Then, in the spring of 1971, King opened for Taylor on a 27-date tour of the US.

She had previously put the music to husband Gerry Goffin's words, but their divorce in 1968 led her to pick up the lyricist's pen. Yet while the confessional singer-songwriter genre allowed people to express their innermost thoughts without embarrassment, it clearly ran counter to her nature. "I don't want people to interpret what I write," she said in 1970. "I have a block against that."

Mind you, she also proclaimed, "I don't want to make LPs, I don't want to be a star"—five months later *Tapestry* was on its way to selling more than 15 million copies. It's a lady's prerogative to change her mind. But this need for privacy, perhaps mindful of her daughters Louise and Sherry, does help explain why she was not keen to attach a name to her songs in terms of inspiration.

When the song was included on *Tapestry*, James Taylor (who else?) was there to add his acoustic guitar to proceedings, as any friend would.

He played on five songs in total, including this one, and also sang backup on this track along with Joni Mitchell. Taylor's own version appeared on his album *Mud Slide Slim and the Blue Horizon*. Taylor's version of "You've Got a Friend" came out as a single in April 1971 and became a huge hit, going all the way to the top of the US charts by July and hitting #4 in the UK.

Taylor tinkered with the words, too. He changed "some loving care" to the more macho "a helping hand," while "Knocking upon your door" for "Knocking at your door" was more of a musical decision to maintain the song's rhythm.

James Taylor on the tour bus in the early 1970s. "You've Got a Friend" may have been Carole King's song, but many thought it was written by Taylor.

In a recorded conversation with producer and Ode Records label chief Lou Adler in 1972, King explained, "When I actually saw James hear it ... and his reaction to it. It then became special to me because of him, you know, and the relationship to him. And it is very meaningful in that way. ...

"His album *Sweet Baby James* was recorded the month before *Tapestry* was recorded, I think. Or even possibly simultaneously. Parts of it were simultaneous. And it was like *Sweet Baby James* flowed over to *Tapestry* and it was like one continuous album in my head. We were all just sitting around playing together and some of them were his songs and some of them were mine."

Musically speaking, a feature of King's writing structure evident in "You've Got a Friend" is to begin in a minor key and then move to the more cheerful major before returning to minor mode. Her songwriting methods varied—sometimes she wrote lyrics first, while other times she wrote the music first or worked with a beat and completed both later. *Tapestry* and the follow-up *Music* also saw her write some tracks in collaboration with lyricist Toni Stern.

James Taylor and Carole King had first performed together at the Troubadour on Santa Monica Boulevard in Hollywood when he had just released his debut album for the Beatles' Apple label and King was testing the water as a solo performer. They returned to the club for a two-week

CAROLE KING started life writing songs for others as part of New York's legendary Brill Building with husband Gerry Goffin. Among these was the first girl-group #1 in 1961, the Shirelles' "Will You Love Me Tomorrow." She hitched a ride on the early-1970s singer-songwriter boom alongside friend James Taylor and came up with a classic of the genre with the 1971 album, *Tapestry*. In 1974 she topped the US album chart for the second time with *Wrap Around Joy*, composed with David Palmer. "I like writing with partners, it gives the material a different dynamic," she explained.

"I don't want people to interpret what I write," King said of her lyric writing. But does that mean Taylor is still free to call winter, spring, summer or fall?

residency in 1971, as Taylor topped the charts and King's *Tapestry* was fast becoming a singer-songwriter bestseller. Thirty-six years later, in November 2007, the duo and members of their band the Section (including mutual friend Danny Kortchmar on guitar) returned to the Troubadour for a six-show run to celebrate the venue's 50th anniversary. Those historic shows were documented on the DVD *Live at the Troubadour.*

In the liner notes, King, 65, states, "What's even more remarkable is that James's and my musical connection and friendship continue to transcend time and place. Whenever we're together, there we are. I feel a tremendous gratitude to be able to share this experience with James, with this fine band, and most of all, with the fans."

Zebulon
Rufus Wainwright

It's never easy for the offspring of famous artists to establish themselves in their own right, but such has been the success of Rufus Wainwright that he has effortlessly eclipsed his parents. Son of multiple-Grammy-winning Loudon Wainwright III and singer Kate McGarrigle, Rufus has established himself as a unique talent, performing ballads, show tunes, and his own opera.

Rufus Wainwright contemplates a lifetime not knowing what happened to Zebulon.

Growing up wasn't easy. Apart from having the burden of "Rufus Is a Tit Man" (see page 96) written for him by a mischievous father, he had to cope with family life that redefined the tag "dysfunctional." At three years old his parents split up, and Kate, Rufus, and sister Martha moved from New York back to live in McGarrigle's native Montreal.

Rufus attended elementary school in Montreal, which is where he met and became friends with Zebulon: "I remember he was a good skier." At this stage Rufus hadn't fully come to terms with being gay. Even at 13 he was involved with mild flirtations with the opposite sex. At an international summer camp in Lyme Regis, Dorset, England, he got himself a girlfriend, "a very Victorian girlfriend. We took long walks along the Cobb [a long harbor wall made famous by Meryl Streep in *The French Lieutenant's Woman*] and drank cider with gypsies in a field."

It was only when he was 14 that he decided to explore an alternative sexuality, by which time Zebulon was no longer a part of his life, the two having moved to different high schools.

> All I need are your eyes
> Your nose was always too big for your face
> Still, it made you look kinda sexy

"I haven't seen him since," admitted Wainwright as he first introduced the song in 2008, which takes the form of a letter to Zebulon. When it was released on the album *All Days Are Nights: Songs for Lulu*, critics seized on its mournful nature and the fact that he describes writing it while his mother was in the hospital with the breast cancer, which would ultimately take her life in 2010.

Rufus admits that songwriting has helped him cope. "I'm always afraid to describe it as a kind of therapeutic process, but nevertheless it was a type of unloading that had to occur due to my personal life with my mother's health or just my professional trials and tribulations. So it was kind of like going to the confessional or something, going to see the priest—the lone walk along the beach. It was my solo time to absorb all of the things that were going on around me."

But "Zebulon" isn't about his mother; it's about "Zebulon." "Really what it's about is pining, or maybe reminiscing about your past, your lost teenage years. As you get further away, they seem more and more beautiful. It's about loving the past a little too much."

Zebulon is about a fondly remembered time and a boy who caught his eye. "I'm just curious to see what he looks like," he confessed when he debuted the song onstage, "so I wrote this song. Maybe he'll pop out of the woodwork."

RUFUS WAINWRIGHT was born in Montreal in 1973, the son of Loudon Wainwright III and Canadian singer Kate McGarrigle. He was the subject of many references in his father's work, including "Rufus Is a Tit Man." With such musical parents his future as a performer was taken for granted, and his first self-titled album came out in May 1998. It wasn't long before an impressed Elton John was referring to him as "the greatest songwriter on the planet." Wainwright acknowledged his homosexuality as a teenager, and his tribute to gay icon Judy Garland, *Rufus Does Judy at Carnegie Hall*, was nominated for a Grammy. It was released concurrently with a live DVD capturing his performance at the London Palladium in 2007. He has diversified into opera—his first, titled *Prima Donna,* premiering in 2009—and, like his father, he has also made his mark on the big screen, most notably in the Martin Scorsese–directed *The Aviator* (2004).

Picture Credits

Alamy: 68. **Anova Image Library:** 12, 20, 50, 52, 58, 59, 66, 81.
Au Hasard Balthazar: 86. **Courtesy of the record company:** 7, 9, 13,
16, 19 (bottom), 23, 25, 28, 33, 36, 39, 41, 44, 49, 51, 53, 57, 61, 62,
63, 65, 67, 69, 72, 79, 82, 85, 87, 88, 93, 94, 95, 96, 100, 103, 104,
109, 111, 113, 115, 118, 121, 124, 129 (bottom), 131 (bottom), 133,
135, 137 (bottom), 140. **Corbis:** 8, 11, 47, 71, 73, 75, 84, 90, 97, 110,
126, 129 (top), 137 (top), 141. **Getty Images:** 19 (top), 22, 29, 45,
48, 55, 64, 77, 89, 92, 98, 101, 105, 107, 108, 114, 120, 122, 128,
130, 131 (top), 134, 136, 142. **Mirrorpix:** 26, 27, 31, 40, 54, 56, 60.
Rex Features: 2, 6, 15, 17, 24, 35, 37, 38, 42, 78, 83, 102, 112, 117,
119, 125, 127, 132, 139.